★ MERLIN ★

About the Author

Gordon Strong has been involved in magick for more than forty years. He is a writer, a teacher, a musician, and a scholar of English literature, Arthurian legend, magick, and the Tarot. He gives talks and conducts workshops on many subjects, including magick and the Tarot. Gordon lives in Somerset, England, where he was born—within sight of the Glastonbury Tor—and grew up.

Please visit his website at www.gordonstrong.co.uk.

·MERLIN·

MASTER OF MAGICK

⊙ ♈ ♈ ♈

△ ⊕ ☽ ♎

GORDON STRONG

Llewellyn Publications
Woodbury, Minnesota

First Edition
First Printing, 2010

Cover illustration © 2009 by Nenad Jakesevic
Cover design by Kevin R. Brown
Llewellyn is a registered trademark of Llewellyn Worldwide, Ltd.

Library of Congress Cataloging-in-Publication Data

Strong, Gordon.
  Merlin : master of magick / Gordon Strong. — 1st ed.
    p. cm.
  Includes bibliographical references.
  ISBN 978-0-7387-1847-7
  1. Merlin (Legendary character) 2. Arthurian romances—History and criticism.
  3. Legends—Great Britain. 4. Wizards in literature. I. Title.
  PN686.M4S76 2010
  398'.45—dc22

                    2009033483

Llewellyn Worldwide does not participate in, endorse, or have any authority or responsibility concerning private business transactions between our authors and the public.
  All mail addressed to the author is forwarded but the publisher cannot, unless specifically instructed by the author, give out an address or phone number.
  Any Internet references contained in this work are current at publication time, but the publisher cannot guarantee that a specific location will continue to be maintained. Please refer to the publisher's website for links to authors' websites and other sources.

Llewellyn Publications
A Division of Llewellyn Worldwide, Ltd.
2143 Wooddale Drive, Dept. 978-0-7387-1847-7
Woodbury, Minnesota 55125-2989, U.S.A.
www.llewellyn.com

Printed in the United States of America

Other books by Gordon Strong

Bride's Mound: Gateway to Avalon (with Jane Marshall)

King Arthur: The Waste Land and the New Age

Stanton Drew and Its Ancient Stone Circles

Tarot Unveiled

Merlin, who knew the range of all their arts,
Had built the King his havens, ships and halls,
Was also Bard, and he knew the starry Heavens;
The people called him wizard.

—TENNYSON

I . . . am also of the race of the Starry Heavens, a spark of
that Mighty Flame, and within me also is that Power . . .
I aspire toward that radiant Source of all Power. O thou,
the Eternal, Whose spark dwells within me, I strive to re-
alise Thee within myself.

—W. E. BUTLER

Do not meddle in the affairs of wizards,
for they are subtle and quick to anger.

—J. R. R. TOLKIEN

Contents

Acknowledgements

First of all I want to thank Alan Richardson for introducing me to my publishers, Llewellyn Worldwide. Alan and I have the kind of friendship which endures because we don't see each other that much. Next, I am deeply grateful to Caterina Fusca, my acquisitions editor at Llewellyn. Through the alchemy of her e-mails, Caterina was always encouraging during the time I was writing this book.

I also owe a debt to that wonderful coterie of writers on magick whose insights have encouraged me over the years. Dion Fortune, W. E. Butler, W. G. Gray, Israel Regardie, Col. Seymour, and Aleister Crowley are, alas, no more and we shall not see their like again. Fortunately, Gareth Knight, Dolores Ashcroft-Nowicki, and R. J. Stewart are still around, and their knowledge was just as valuable to my research.

Finally, I want to thank my beloved partner, Shama, for just being there. Her presence enhances everything in my life.

* Introduction *

Merlin—as magnificent in myth as in reality—was the father of magick and the equal of kings. For those involved in magick and those others who might just be curious about what makes up the magickal world, Merlin remains the archetypal magician. He is the first and the best—just as the Beatles have that stature in pop music. His magick has a particular ambiance, solid and earthy, yet at the same time oozing endless mystery—part of the world and yet not quite.

If he is chronicling the life of a man who constantly hovers between myth and reality, the writer must adopt an approach that best suits his subject. If that subject is also a magician, then any biographer must adopt a strategy akin to playing three-dimensional chess. A linear account of a character whose nature tends toward constantly hopping from one reality plane to another would not do justice to Merlin. More importantly, the reader would not be given the chance to fully embrace a wizard in all his wondrous diversity. Thus, in this narrative, shifts in time and space occur, and the writer feels this should be so. Any difficulties of interpretation that the reader might experience will be far outweighed by his gaining a deeper understanding of Merlin.

Not for Merlin the temple and the orchestrated ritual; that would be too close to the conventions of the court and the monastery to suit his temperament. Although he is well aware of the power of words, as his lyrical prophecies show, he is a man of inspiration. The spirit of the Bard is in him, and like the great English Romantic poets of the nineteenth century—Byron, Shelley, and Keats—he seeks freedom above everything else. For Merlin, true liberty can be found only in the wildest and most distant corners of this or any other world. Although he has a high profile in the Arthurian tales, he has too a love of solitude.

Merlin is a man of the forest and the mountain peaks. He is never happier than when surveying the distant horizon of a world that, in magickal terms, his own hand helped to form. The power that is deep within the earth sustains him, and he frequents sacred places where that energy, as the magician knows only too well, is at its strongest. Merlin would have understood the current predilection for visiting megalithic monuments and revering ancient ways. He is a figure who would feel comfortable with the ideals of the New Age. This is not because he was 'the first shaman', a title which scarcely does him justice, but because he is man as a *sentient being*. We are surrounded in the twenty-first century by an arid and barren materialism. By sharing the vision of Merlin, we realise that the world is still a place of wonder, joy, and infinite potential.

My own childhood was lived in the moorlands of Somerset, a few miles from Glastonbury. I know that I always regarded the land as being imbued with magick. The sky above, the flowing waters, and every creature that had its home there was somehow sacred. I saw, as did Blake, 'eternity in a grain of sand'. Then, I would not have been able to articulate such feelings, nor would I have felt the need to. But even as a child I was aware of the universal force that binds creation together. To me that power was not 'God'—that would have been far too glib a view. That might was best seen in the towering waves, heard in the roar of the wind, and reflected in the countless stars. I was a wolf, alone in the wilds, as Merlin himself was for a time.

The story of Merlin is the story of magick, and the magician of every age imbibes some of his spirit. While writing of his life, I realised that *every* aspect of magick is in Merlin. His every moment was dedicated to his calling, and he was a pioneer, inventor, and virtuoso of the magickal art. The Western Magical Tradition would not exist without Merlin, and that in itself is enough for us to be grateful to the old wizard. More than that, he represents the mighty imagination and the magnificent universe. To me, he is a mentor and, I like to think, a friend. Not that we should ever take liberties with the ones we love, particularly men of magick—that would be asking for trouble.

Some of my readers may be puzzled by my spelling of the word *magick*. I use that form so as not to confuse the esoteric art with *magic*, which is *conjuring* or *léger de main* (sleight of hand). Aleister Crowley promoted this archaic form and also suggested a numerological explanation for it based on the value of the letter k, the thirteenth letter of the alphabet. The keen student is quite welcome to pursue the rest of Crowley's thesis on this point, and with my blessing.

Gordon Strong
Portishead, England
November 2008

∗ Portrait of a Wizard ∗

It [magick] can make the clouds rain and the sun shine, it can bring favour or disgrace, it can revive the dead and kill the living, it can change a man's shape and make him into a bird or a beast. Its very secrecy leads to the possibilities of dreams and fancies.

—DR. G. STORMS

Ancient Magick

In Atlantis or ancient Egypt, there may have been greater magicians than Merlin, but their names have not come down to us. In the West, Merlin is the first practitioner of the magickal art. Like King Arthur, Merlin is a significant player in the British psyche. In this *unconscious realm* of Britain reside our ancient heroes. It is an invisible world, existing side by side with the conscious plane, and has within it the roots of all the Western Magical Tradition. Merlin is the steward of the power that flows from that mystical plane into the upper world.

As soon as human beings became aware of the world, they tried to *understand* the nature of their existence. They reflected upon the human condition, and continue to do so. The philosophers of ancient Greece asked the same questions as our Neolithic ancestors, and in the twenty-first century we keep asking them. In Great Britain our predecessors built stone circles, patterns constructed with a view to making sense of the universe. And as soon as humans began to think, they practised magick. Man was a pragmatic creature and hunting was his main preoccupation, so he set about finding ways of attracting his prey. He did that by assuming the form of the stag or the wild boar, and by becoming them in his imagination he knew them better on the conscious plane. Thus, magick was originally about sharing valuable insights with those around you.

The lives of those before the age of Merlin were determined by the gods, and the voices of those gods. These they heard within themselves. They would not have understood the separation of conscious and unconscious, an idea upheld by modern people. Paleolithic and Neolithic people were spurred into action by the dictates of the divine presence. They were not the 'savages' that Victorian archaeologists were so fond of depicting, but were engaged upon their own survival along with their animal neighbours. When came *thought* also came the first magick, as human beings wished to control what they experienced. Their desires would have been simple—success at hunting or a plentiful harvest.

A landscape completely untouched and unspoiled—it is almost impossible to imagine the world of the ancients, living as we do, surrounded by all the changes people have made to the environment. And at what cost to our spiritual lives! In five millennia the magnetic field surrounding Earth has been reduced by at least 50 percent. This diminishing of its aura accounts for the loss of the 'sixth sense', resulting in only a minority having true awareness. We may have gained through the harnessing of natural energies, but we have lost our ability to tune in to our surroundings and be at one with them. A state of oneness with the world is no longer a given as it once was.

In our own 'reasoned' age, magick has the disadvantage of not being quantifiable. It admits the existence of the unknown, and thus, to the scientist, loses any authority that the discipline once had. If an attempt is made to reproduce the supernatural in laboratory conditions, it will simply not play along. Polarity is at the heart of magick, shaping its nature and fuelling its power. The magician walks a tightrope between the inner and outer worlds. Always keeping in mind that he knows, and at the same time does not know, he is aware of the paradox that allows him to pass beyond the veil. To regard this world with awe and wonder is an approach far more likely to result in the universe sharing its secrets. People are too often inclined to arrogantly declare that they know everything there is to know. Dion Fortune defined magick as 'the ability to control natural forces at will'. A magician of a succeeding generation, Bill Gray, proposed that to *accept* the limitations of our existence was an admission of defeat. It was Gray's view that if we are the 'crown of creation' we should busy ourselves with working miracles. Merlin would have certainly agreed with that view.

First, let us understand the distinction between the *mystic* and the *magician*. The former is content to 'let it all happen'; the latter acts to achieve certain ends by using the will. It has to be said that mysticism might be the ultimate goal of the magician as it has within it an acceptance of the Divine Will. On two significant occasions in his life Merlin appears to totally surrender his will, but things are never quite what they seem to be. The gift of magick that is bestowed by the Higher Powers is in the nature of a loan. The magician knows this and uses his power fittingly—ultimately to do good.

Even the most experienced magician can fail in a magickal undertaking or make a wrong decision. What *you* want must be in accord with *what the universe wants*. If the gods are against you there is nothing you can do about it. It might be that you have simply chosen the wrong moment or you have asked for the wrong thing. The Higher Power is the modus operandi of the Divine Will—that which determines every outcome. Sometimes it may be right that the magician fails in some endeavour, the reason for this he or anyone else cannot possibly know. He must simply accept what has happened and continue on his path without regret, and with a lightness of heart.

The magician must cultivate a ruthless indifference to what happens in the world so that his power is never perverted or weakened by personal considerations. 'Be in the world but not of it' as the Buddhist maxim tells us. Powers greater than man or magician are the final arbiter in this existence. By realizing the temporal nature of all things, the magician remains in harmony with the Universe. 'Nothing exists, nothing has ever existed, nothing will ever exist' is another Eastern wisdom. Magick never claims to be able to alter destiny; it merely suggests that, 'if we do *this* in *that* order, we will have a clearer idea of the nature of the divine'. Hence the magickal principle: As *above so below*.

Image and Myth

Since the advent of cartoons and comics, Merlin—as the most celebrated and easily identifiable wizard of magickal lore—has been a gift to the artist and animator. Wand in hand, the pointed hat always at a bizarre angle and covered in stars, he trips over his voluminous robes straight into our hearts. The image might not be quite as ridiculous as it seems, for Merlin is a denizen of the stars and Moon, and his hat belongs to the witch. This familiar design is a combination of the cone and the circle, the directed power of the sacred round or ring. The design originates in Persia where the *Magi* (might, mighty) were the priests of the Zoroastrian religion. They apparently possessed all the necessary skills and virtues of the successful magician of any age. Their badge of office was a tall, conical hat, and thus was the tradition created.

The *Cone of Power* was a powerful ritual that was performed by a great number of witches, notably on two occasions in English history. Both times the purpose was to forestall invasion of these islands—a ploy which fortunately succeeded. In 1588 the Spanish Armada was wrecked by storms, supposedly evoked by occult means, and in 1940 the threat of invasion by Nazi Germany was thwarted by the same powers. As a result, both Philip of Spain and Hitler, respectively, abandoned any ambitions to conquer England.

The *Oxford English Dictionary* defines *wizard* as a 'person who affects seeming impossibilities . . . ' To attain this, Merlin has one foot in heaven, the other on the earth. Between two worlds is the place where magick lies, and as the Tarot card of the Magician depicts so well, Merlin brings power from above to the earthly plane below. Never has the notion of the macrocosm and microcosm been as ably demonstrated as when Merlin performs, so effortlessly, every kind of magick. He also employs the power of the natural world, working from *within and without* and making his magick, such as when he controls the skies, so awesome and dramatic.

'Spectacular' is the quality we associate with him, that and limitless power. Merlin is the archetypal magician; he makes the impossible possible. The techniques that most magicians spend a lifetime to acquire were part of his mystical armoury, almost from birth. Merlin will always be remembered as a performer, one who acts out his moods. He is the master of dramatic illusion because he generates confidence and conviction, qualities essential for any magician. People are naturally attracted to magick and many of them for entirely the wrong reasons. Some believe it to be glamorous or dangerous, while others think it is all pink crystals and incense; it is neither of these things.

Of his appearance, we are told that the wolf is the familiar of Merlin, and he clothes himself in wolf skin. The wolf is a powerful totemic creature. The Turkic shamans believed that their people were the descendants of wolves.

The Plains Indians believed that the wolf was sacred to the direction of the west, that of water and the Goddess. Romulus and Remus, the founders of Rome, were saved as babes when they were suckled by a she-wolf. The animal is sacred to Mars, the planet that rules Aries and Scorpio, the most independent of the signs of the zodiac. The wolf is also depicted as the star Sirius (from the Greek *seirios*, 'glowing'). It is the brightest star in the night sky and many myths are associated with it. In the Norse tradition it is 'Loki's torch'. The appellation of the 'Dog Star' may have been a confusion with its real origins, for the Chinese call it the 'Celestial Wolf' and to the North American tribe of the Pawnee it is the 'Wolf Star'. The wolves Geri and Freki were Odin's faithful companions and reputedly of 'good omen'.

The sight of the dying wolf in winter is an omen of change for Merlin; it represents the casting off of his old personality and his adopting of the new. The direction of winter is associated with the north, the element of Earth, and the domain of the ancestors. Merlin will gain greater wisdom from every change he undergoes in his life. The wolf is the precursor of the domesticated dog who displays affection and loyalty to its master. In a poignant twist, his master will be his mistress, as we shall later discover! Much may be gained from contemplation of the little white dog in the Fool card of the Tarot. Is he encouraging humanity to make a leap into the unknown, or is he barking a warning before it is too late?

Merlin carries a cudgel, with which he amuses himself by striking it against oak trees. Inevitably he loves animals more than men, whom he often sees as vicious and stupid. If people attempt to deceive him, his contempt quickly turns to wrath. Yet he has an air of modesty about him and never wishes to dominate others or seek their praise. Do we regard his resigned attitude to the world as being typically 'English'? It is tempting to see Merlin as the first English eccentric, one step away from a modern Merlin who might wear carpet slippers and smoke a pipe. We must remember that regarding the 'English' as a separate race is a mistake. They originate in Jutland, Angeln, and Lower Saxony; if anything, the 'English' are German.

Merlin wishes to embrace humanity and its ways, and aid people in their progress. He is an amiable fellow and never stands aloof from the simple and the sincere. Yet, like Castaneda's Don Juan, he remains 'impeccable'. This way, nothing weakens his power, for he neither allows anybody or anything to draw upon his magickal energy. Like all magicians, Merlin has the ability to be invisible. He attains this end by drawing in his aura so much to himself that it hardly exists. Thus, he is simply not noticed. Like cats, who always appear to be purposeful, even when sleeping, Merlin is always *aware*. The price he pays is not being able to share the bonds of ordinary friendship. Those who would take up the esoteric path have chosen a calling which is not part of 'society'. For the magician, ordinary intimacy is rare, even in the company of his own kind.

Heritage

In the great magickal lineage, Merlin succeeds Thoth. We would not wish to exclude Solomon from this occult pedigree, but it can be fairly said that his reputation as a Hebrew monarch far outweighs his role as a practitioner of magick. His building of the Temple to house the Ark of the Covenant is admirable, but his apparent habit of evoking demons to aid that work seems more questionable. Thoth employs his reason to guide the 'Ship of Life' which is a symbolic representation of Isis. She is his magickal pupil and brings her learning to the Great Unconscious where magick now resides. This state also encompasses humanity and nature, and Isis is also responsible for the manifestation of all form, for her spirit is in every atom of the universe.

In the Egyptian Book of the Dead, Isis is described as 'she who gives birth to heaven and earth'. Without Isis nothing would be seen, as actual existence resides within her. She is also known, among many other titles, as the Queen of Heaven, The One Who is All, Star of the Sea, and Mother of the Gods. There is much of Hathor, her predecessor, in the nature of Isis, and she once adopted the former's headdress of two horns surrounding a solar disc as her own. In later Egyptian creeds, Isis is the mother of Horus rather than Hathor. It is important to understand that when he is with Isis, Thoth exchanges her female energy with his own male power. Later, when Thoth adopts Maat, or Seshat, as his consort, his magickal union is complete. His partner is known as *Mistress of the House of Books*. She is often seen dressed in cheetah or leopard hide to represent the stars in the night sky.

Isis is the daughter of Geb, god of the Earth, and Nut, goddess of the sky. She can be seen as inheriting the crown of Wadjet, the primal protector of all Egypt, who is a snake-headed goddess, sometimes even depicted as a snake with a female head. Wadjet is in turn closely associated with Bast or Bastet, the lioness-headed deity who is protector of Ra and goddess of the Sun. This 'Lady of Flame' blasts fire at the enemies of Ra much as the cobra spits poison. Sekhmet is the later, more well-known form of the Sun goddess. She retains an echo of Wadjet in the snake that is poised above her leonine features. The 'Lady of Flame' becomes the 'Eye of Ra', as Thoth is the 'Voice of Ra'.

The tale of Osiris, the brother/husband of Isis who is dismembered by Seth, culminates when Isis, aided by Thoth, restores his body to a whole. Thus Thoth is the teacher of Isis, yet she completes her magickal knowledge by covertly learning the sacred name of Ra and by this means inheriting his magickal gifts. Wadjet and Serket, the scorpion goddess, gave Isis a comprehensive array of magickal skills. Her son Horus was a powerful magickal being also, and in evocations of Isis the two are often merged. When Horus was poisoned by his enemies, Ra sent Thoth to cure him. As a result Isis vowed that she would heal any mortal who in suffering made an appeal to her. Isis is the goddess of rebirth and reincarnation and thus no stranger to the underworld. She is also *guardian of the veil*, which makes her role so significant in the history of magick. The shrine of Isis carries this inscription, 'I am all that hath been, and is, and shall be; and my veil no mortal has hitherto raised'. Intriguingly, the Goddess raises the veil herself at the time of the Full Moon, as those who practice magick know only too well.

Merlin originates from a time when the world was the domain of gods and half-formed creatures, a time before *Homo sapiens* loomed so large in the cosmic equation. Chaos, when it finally becomes a manifested state, is described as the 'Great Sea'. The 'divine thought' is named the Great Silence. From these two states were born the Old Gods. We may profitably consider how these primeval deities reflect human consciousness. The first Mystery Schools, having no other divine material to work upon, attempted to draw together earth, mind, and man to create a synthesis that would represent an empirical and transcendental intelligence.

Four aspects of human consciousness were proposed. First, are the rulers of natural forces—the Sun, the Moon, the tides, and the weather. Second are the supernatural beings who occupied the earth in prehistoric times. Traces of this power still remain, and can be tapped by authentic Pagan practices. *Paganus* means 'country dweller', so it is inevitable that the first recognised deity will be the Earth Mother. Female statuettes dating from many thousands of years ago have been discovered in various parts of the world by archaeologists. We do not know who these figures represent, but the theme of fertility and the great mother is graphically depicted in their design. Later, Isis will become the Goddess in her sublime incarnation. The lunar vibration was the foundation of what was to be known as witchcraft, the most ancient of all magickal practice. Thirdly, there are deities of the seasons and the cardinal directions. From the earliest times the changes in the year were marked with great ceremony. Thoth, Ra, Isis, and Geb from the Egyptian pantheon were frequently used for this purpose by members of the Golden Dawn. The adoption of the four Archangels to represent the different character of the cardinal directions is relatively modern, yet these powerful officers of Heaven are very effective in ritual. Finally we must also consider human emotions, assumed to be affected by the mood of the gods. Offering sacrifices to placate and honour deities is a practice so old as to be almost integral to the spiritual development of humanity.

Prophet and Bard

Merlin is Hermes, Loki, Woden, and even Gwyn Ap Nudd—the King of the Fairies. From trickster to prophet, Magus to Holy Fool, his character has endless twists and turns. He is jester, prophet, and bard; a healer, adviser, and servant of gods—and the Goddess. Before the first century BCE, a distinct 'British' culture existed in these islands, shown by the rivers Clyde and Thames, names which bear no etymological link to Celtic languages. Tracing the recorded accounts of Merlin leads us inevitably to Geoffrey of Monmouth, a twelfth-century bishop and Latin scholar who wrote several accounts of early British history. These include the *Vita Merlini*, written between 1149 and 1151, which gave our wizard the titles *Merlin Ambrosius*, *Emrys*, and *Myrddin*. *Merlinus* is favoured over *Merdinu*, because the latter in the French language is too close to a vulgar pun. The first name Britain owned before it was settled was *Myrddin's Precinct*. After this, according to *The White Book of Rhydderch*, it was named *Merdin*—'the holy isle' or the 'Honey Isle of Beli'. The conquest by Prydain, son of Aedd the Great, then led to the country being renamed the *Island of Prydain*. In Welsh history Merlin is depicted as a wild man from Carmarthen, and in Scotland he is simply known as *Merlin Calidonus*.

Merlin reflects many of the hallmarks of Celtic magick, such as shapeshifting, but he too is of another age. Merlin is surrounded—as is Gandalf, his fictional counterpart—by an air of melancholy. He is aware that another age, that of Christianity, is about to succeed his own Pagan world. Like Arthur, Merlin will return once again to advise and protect us, but only if our faith in him remains intact. To his contemporaries Merlin was renowned for his gift of prophecy. Let us now examine this gift.

In 368 BCE Plato wrote in the *Phaedrus*, 'the first prophecies were the words of an oak'. He advised people to 'listen to an oak or a stone, so long as it was telling the truth'. As well as using the technique of scrying, the prophecies of Merlin were based upon his astrological/astronomical observations.

Regarding the future of Logres, the Arthurian kingdom, Merlin predicts the death of Arthur—'The Mighty Lion shall be overthrown', and that of Gawain. Yet these are almost domestic issues compared to the vast amount of prophetic material collected by Geoffrey of Monmouth. This part of the text in *Vita Merlini* is largely expressed in apocalyptic terms— 'Therefore shall the mountains be levelled as the valleys, and the rivers of the valleys shall run with blood'. What is significant is not the rhetoric but the authenticity of the voice—it is an original history. The sentiments are very similar in tone to the Welsh *Myrddin* poems of the sixth century, suggesting that this is the authentic voice of the wizard Merlin.

It is said of the manner in which the prophecies were written that Merlin had merely to trace his fingers over the letters for them to become visible. It must be said that even such an impressive method as that cannot serve to alter destiny one jot. The role of Merlin seems to be only to advise and so to aid his fellow man. Merlin has also made an unspoken vow to the powers concerning his ability to exercise his art. He is determined that his prophecies will not be mere entertainment, and he knows that the need for divination must be genuine, or the ability to reveal any mystery will disappear. Merlin is devoted to the Heavens that bestow the power of magick upon him. He uses this power to facilitate the Divine Will upon the Earth. In return, Merlin is given the power to maintain his inner resolve, for *will* is essential to practise magick. As we will discover, this resolve will be severely tested.

As he observed the Heavens, Merlin would see the phases of the Moon and the patterning of the stars. Merlin's 'magickal reality' was akin to his first perceptions of cosmology and, as we shall discover, he added significantly to the total of knowledge possessed by the ancients. In ancient Greece Apollo's medium would sit above a fissure in the earth to contact the earth power below. In the same way Merlin's power undoubtedly came from channeling magnetic earth currents. This explains Merlin's enthusiasm for predicting lunar eclipses, which dynamically affect both the earth and water on the planet. Earth is the static element and *contains* water until the latter can be restrained no longer. As the Summer Solstice is a productive time for the medium, so the Winter Solstice is an important event for the magician. At this time the Sun is in Capricorn and the Moon in its own sign of Cancer; at such a time much can be done to refine the self, removing unwanted energies in order to be ready to begin the new year.

Merlin may also have been the figure Taliesin (Radiant Brow), later bard to King Arthur. One of Taliesin's poems even has the line, 'Johannes the diviner called me Myrrhdin . . .'. Taliesin was either the son or the servant of Cerridwen. In the ancient tale three drops of liquid were spilt from the sacred Cauldron onto his hand, which he duly licked and gained wisdom. As wonderful as that tale is his own verse:

I existed as a multitude of things.
Before I was given substance,

I was a shadowy sword held in the right hand,
I believe in that which can be seen,
But I was a tear drop in the air,
I was the most brilliant of all the galaxy of stars.
I was a word in a thousand words.
I was the original book.
I was a beam of light . . . [1]

---

1. Quoted in Ronald Millar, Will the Real King Arthur Please Stand Up?
   (London: Cassell, 1978), p. 80.

* An Extraordinary *
Coming

Because I am dark and always shall be, let my book be dark and mysterious in those places where I will not show myself.

MERLIN—MEDIEVAL TEXT

Devil and Virgin

Like the birth of Arthur, Merlin's arrival in this world is also shrouded in mystery and the shadows of the Otherworld. Was he the child of a princess (the daughter of King Conaan), or the grandson of another monarch—the King of Demetia? It was also said that his father was the element of Air, who could make earthly women conceive by merely breathing upon them. Some say Merlin's mother was a nun named Aldan, his father a devil. Others insisted that his parents were Taranis the thunder god and Cerridwen, though her supposed husband was Tegid Foel, the tutelary deity of Bala Lake in Gwynedd, North Wales. She had two sons: Morfran, who is hideous, and one other who becomes Taliesin the Bard. It is the latter who is often considered to be the alter ego of Merlin. Cerridwen owned the famous Cauldron, so Merlin's association with the artefact that later became the Grail begins early.

Stories abound of Merlin narrowly escaping death as a babe—in a similar scenario, it must be said, to the infant Christ escaping the cruel decree of Herod to slay the first born of Bethlehem. A similar tale is also told of the Celtic Apollo, Mabon, and of Lug, another Celtic deity of whom we shall hear more as the story of Merlin unfolds. From being akin to the Saviour, accusations then abound as to Merlin being the Antichrist. In the *Merlin* of Robert de Boron, Merlin is once again conceived by a virgin as part of a plot by the denizens of Hell. The scheme is foiled when the mother is given the sign of the cross during her pregnancy, resulting in the child being born with a dual nature. From the devils he receives the power to know the past, 'those things which had been, and done, and said, and gone' and the pelt of a wolf. From Heaven he receives the power of divination.

All this did not prevent Merlin's later reputation as a *daimon* gaining ground. Originally meaning 'divine power' or 'spirit of inspiration', the ever-vigilant Christian Church transformed the word into *demon*—'malignant entity'. It seems that the denizens of the Dark Ages were never quite sure if Merlin was the son of the devil or the servant of God.

Like Melchizedek of Salem, who has no earthly home and exists only on the inner planes, Merlin is 'without beginning or end'. He has, as we would expect from a master of illusion, an air of 'now you see me—now you don't'. He will always remain controversial, never quite meeting with approval and never seeking it either. He is cunning like the fox, and as much an outlaw. But we must never forget that in *magickal terms* he represents wisdom, and although one of the lesser grades, the greater mysteries being the Grail and the Quest, he is on a par with Arthur in the Tales. It is apparent that after Merlin has progressed along the spiritual path, he actually becomes the essence of the Grail.

The character of Merlin is, like the essence of magick, a paradox. His easy embracing of the feminine or Goddess energy, what the philosopher Jung would later name the *anima*, indicates that he may once have been nurtured by a nature goddess himself. The Goddess is *form*, the fabric of the universe. Knowing this, the magician is able to evoke her power and alter the nature of his own form. He becomes so fluid that he may actually pass through solid objects as if he was invisible. To assume the form of other creatures is a talent attributed to the witch and the shaman. The magician may also make the world disappear by enticing the Goddess to sleep. The eternal remains, but the temporal is no longer there. A magician is not divine but he is the closest to a god that a person may be. Merlin is never, like ordinary mortals, restrained by limits of time and space. He may too have a reputation for being a charlatan, madman, and even a murderer, but it makes little difference; it is what he achieves as a wanderer, guide, and guardian of kings that is important.

We should never delude ourselves into thinking that we 'know' anything—we cannot ever be *certain* that what we perceive is 'real'. Neither is understanding gained by attempting to decide what is 'right' or 'wrong'. Jung reasoned that the human mind oscillated between sense and nonsense, not an infallible perception of right and wrong. Moral judgment alone often leads to grave error and worse. *Thought* is in itself a powerful weapon—ruled by the element of Air and symbolized by the sword—and thought forms can be either creative or destructive. The magician uses the power of thought projection when he creates an inner world, but only after he has rigorously trained his mind. If any negative or fearful thoughts enter there he dismisses them immediately. Morbidity has no place in the world of the magician; his aura is one of the brightest light. Illumination may attract its opposite—darkness— but the magician has the courage and the stamina to face any challenge to his calling. He knows that the inner light he has gained has the power to banish any shadow that may surround him.

Human beings are capable of great achievements, but too easily do we believe we have destiny at our command. Our conclusions should be tempered by a consideration that there exists a great unknown—forces that exist, unknown and unseen, and patently unwilling to do our bidding. To the Celt all living things were linked in a kaleidoscope of form and feeling. The 'carpet pages', the ornately embellished initial letters in the Book of Kells, depict this with grace and flair. Fishes become humans, who in their turn become trees and clouds—all is one and much the better for it.

Earth Spirits

Merlin has much in common with Lugh, a Celtic deity who has in turn much of Mercury about him. Lugh has many talents, and describes himself as a wright, a champion, a swordsman, harpist, hero, poet, historian, and sorcerer. His name may derive from a root word meaning 'flashing light', or if it is *lonnbeimnech*, 'fierce striker'. The root of his name might also be *lugios*, which has among other meanings 'bond' and 'binding oath'. Mercury is the god of commerce and business contracts. Lugh gave the Celtic people *Lughnasadh*, one of the Quarter Days, celebrated on the first day of August. The Lammas festival is a harvest festival. It is said that Lugh wrested the harvest from the underworld and saved it for the people of the earth. His weapons are depicted in the Heavens; his sling rod is the Rainbow and his chain the Milky Way. By far the most celebrated of these arms is *Brionac*, his spear. Fire flashes from it in battle and the enemy is no match for its power. Brionac is so fierce, even of its own accord, that to calm it the weapon must be drugged with poppy seeds. Lugh also owns a magic hound which causes water to change into mead or wine if the animal bathes in a spring.

The association of Merlin with Druidry may be solely attributed to an honorary title he is supposed to have held at the Temple of Lleu or Mabon, the Celtic Apollo. There he was a prophet and healer and appointed Chief Druid, a rank that gave him the right to preside at the inauguration of kings. The less fortunate legacy of this position was to inherit the 'Threefold Death' which was assigned to the avatar of Lleu. Thus, being considered the incarnation of the 'Divine King' apparently sealed the fate of Merlin. We shall learn more of the notion of sacrifice and all that it entails, and also the manner of Merlin's death when we study the end of his life. It is as well to remember that the 'Threefold Death' was associated closely with kings and priests, the two earthly roles that manifest the Divine Will.

Who was the teacher of Merlin? Did he learn his magick from the Masters of the Inner Planes as his modern magickal counterpart is wont to do? The claim to have personal guardians and guides, usually a Tibetan monk or the ubiquitous Native American shaman, is a particular phenomenon of our time. Contrast these benign beings with the entity who Merlin may have encountered—a creature of awe and terror. And not really a 'being' at all in the accepted sense, more an overwhelming 'presence', such as that experienced by 'sensitives'. Given that Merlin's great affinity is with earth spirits, this one would have been the mother and father of all things associated with that element in its grossest manifestation.

Satyrs, dryads, sprites, and their ilk seem to flit harmlessly about the sylvan glades of Britain, yet lurking in the darkest shadows is a force, visible yet invisible. It can be seen among the rocks in the mountains, giving to them almost human features. In the sky after a storm and felt on the shore at dusk, this presence has lingered from the dawn of creation. It comes from a time when the gods before the gods ruled. The spirit of Merlin was there at the dawn of our world. He is eternal because he occupies a physical world and a magickal world simultaneously.

Merlin is both the Magician and the Fool, and these two Tarot cards, the Magician and the Fool, represent the two paths from *Kether*, the Crown at the head of the Tree of Life. Study first the image of the Tarot Magician, standing at his magickal table, the altar, between the blooms of Heaven and the flowers of the earth which he has manifested. The Divine Power flows for eternity around the lemniscate, the symbol of infinity, above him. It crackles like lightning around the wand he holds aloft in his right hand, is sent through the Sephiroth of Tiphareth that is the magician's heart, to emerge from the fingers of the left hand which he is pointing towards the earth. The slight smile that hovers around his features hints that on one level he is simply enjoying the experience. He is *detached* from what he is doing and yet totally involved—that is yet another *magickal paradox*, one essential to those who would understand the nature of magick.

The other card, the Fool, is an allegory of magickal energy. It is the 'right' moment—the present, combining the tantric and ultimately the unrepeatable—the elusive. The beautifully turned-out figure steps, not blindly but knowingly, from the security of the solid earth into the abyss below. The plane he enters is the abode of power, and he is at one with that power already. With his leap into the unknown, the Fool has become so much part of the universe that he is every part of it. The Fool is the *phenomenal* state challenging the *causal*. The affinity between the Tarot cards of the Magician and the Fool is very apparent. The Fool is the *essence of magick*—its actual *power*, while the Magician is aware that *every* act is a magickal act. Possessing that knowledge separates him from his ordinary fellows.

The Fool is poised on the edge of the abyss, as is all humanity. What makes *him* different is his total control over his situation. The Magician too has that equilibrium, one that comes from knowing intimately two worlds. For these two figures, the outcome of their endeavours will always be successful. They have been chosen by the *Masters of the Inner Planes* to bring the perfection of Heaven to the chaos of Earth, and the one always reflects the other.

Whether Arthur and Merlin are merely heroes of folklore or real personages is a question that is often asked of the historian and also the student of metaphysics. Both schools of belief have gained ascendancy at different times. The magician holds that both views are right! Another paradox, that of denial and affirmation, comes into play—the truth is a combination of both ideas. We are dwelling in the world of archetypes and it is here, as Jung confirmed, that the reality of the unconscious holds sway. The Inner Planes offer a valid truth as much as does the conscious plane, and to understand magick we must embrace this view.

Merlin Mercurius

Knowing about Merlin actually brings us nearer to understanding the ways of the Goddess. Her unfettered spirit is embraced by Merlin. He has an affinity with the Roman deity Minerva in his closeness to the heart of creation. He is the first magician to draw on both the *anima* and the *animus* within the psyche. Merlin is always the pragmatist; he is not a prototype of the twentieth-century 'new man'. His magickal predecessors worked only with the will, but Merlin is shrewd enough to realise that the power of manifestation will always be exclusively in the domain of the Goddess. She is *form*—that is the way that she is able to render the divine energy—while the 'god' energy is always potential. The Qabalah illustrates this principle through the path that lies between Chokmah and Binah. It is represented by the Tarot card of the Empress, and even more succinctly, the path that connects Netzach and Hod is the Falling Tower.

Though it is beyond the bounds of this work to include a treatise upon the Qabalah, those who wish to study this system of transcendental knowledge can only increase their occult knowledge.

The Priestess has practised her magick in the Temple since ancient times. The most telling depiction of her resides in The High Priestess card of the Tarot. Looking particularly knowing, as the Magician appears to be equally enigmatic, Isis, as the figure undoubtedly is, sits before the veil. It is a curtain decorated with a design of pomegranates and represents simultaneously desire for knowledge and the netherworld. The veil hides what is beyond, but what can just be seen in Pamela Colman Smith's masterly design is an endless stretch of water. It appears to be calm on the surface, but as we all know beneath the waves are always powerful and mysterious, ever-changing currents. The key to every puzzle is to be found beyond the veil, and also the way to rectify every dilemma. So, it is a place of fascination and delight as well as wisdom. It is also where the Magus resides. Having gained such knowledge of the Inner Planes that there is nothing he does not comprehend, he passes into this place of ultimate knowledge.

We perceive the world in a certain way, and for the majority that particular view determines how it might be. It is impossible to perceive others except through our own eyes; we are also a mirror, and often see 'through a glass darkly'. But to dwell for too long upon these things is to become prey to the world of illusions yet again. We cannot know the purpose of existence, as that knowledge is not bequeathed to us. Better to employ ourselves wholeheartedly in the rhythm of life. By keeping in time with the universe we are part of it, yet we maintain that essential distance that will sustain us.

The 'mass consciousness' is always very different from the *universal mind*. The latter is a manifestation of the Divine Will and exists, not in the material sense, below or beyond the consensus of reality that the majority embrace. It exists separately from that material world, the superficial appearance of things, but is still the force that determines what actually happens. Watch how things in the world suddenly change! Triumphs and disasters occur at every level and in every sphere of life. These events appear to be almost arbitrary. This is why the average person can often see no real *meaning* in life. He may turn to religion, which will be only too willing to provide him with answers, but he knows his soul is never completely satisfied. What he cannot perceive is the ebb and flow of existence—the divine rhythm. Man tries to control the material world and inevitably fails most of the time. He will not acknowledge these hidden rhythms in the way that his ancestors did. In fact, his ancestors were much wiser than he is. The modern mindset cannot abide changes that cannot be predicted or controlled.

We exist in a world of three dimensions, though we might just as easily have inherited an existence that took place in four dimensions. If the laws of physics were suddenly reversed or removed, the conscious world would appear as the unconscious. On the Inner Planes it is the magician who sets the rules of the game. The magician is not subject to any conception of time, and therefore in having mastery of the moment he can decide the nature of the moment. As the shepherd knows every cloud in the sky, so does the magician know every detail of the magickal landscape. But this knowing does not come without knowledge and experience. Although our technological and 'tick the right box' age would have us believe it is possible to acquire skills and understanding instantly, it is simply not so. The acid test of a magician is whether he can do magick or not.

Trickster

Clowning of some kind should always precede the act of prayer. Laughter frees us from the cage of convention and sets free the uncanny and the unpredictable. Humour is a kind of birth, and with all that entails. We cry with laughter when cosmic mirth overwhelms us. The Native American tradition cites the coyote as the 'Trickster Hero' who like Prometheus stole fire for humanity, but who also could bring floods to dampen their spirits. The latter recalls Epimetheus, the brother of Prometheus, who constantly makes the wrong decision. A spirit of the night, he has the power to lead the lost out of danger, although he is never to be entirely trusted. The character of Merlin is very similar, for he is like Hermes, inclined to be cunning and not always honest. Hermes is the god of thieves. The story of Hermes and his brother Apollo casts an interesting light on the similarities between Merlin and the Mercurial god.

The babe Hermes stole the cattle of Apollo and hid them in a cave. He caught and killed a tortoise, and using the intestines from one of the stolen cows, fashioned the first lyre. When Apollo protested to Zeus about the theft of his cattle, Hermes was ordered to return them. Hermes cleverly beguiled Apollo with the music of the lyre, and later they agreed to exchange the instrument for his cattle. Later still, Hermes obtained the Caduceus from Apollo in exchange for another musical instrument—the flute. If we substitute King Arthur for Apollo, which is perfectly plausible as they are both Sun gods, we have an earthly version of the brotherly love of the two deities. Hermes is the offspring of Zeus, who, like Taranis and his claps of thunder, has lightning bolts at his disposal. The Mother of Hermes is Gaea, who is the spirit of the World. Thus the earthly connection is made.

We cannot accuse Merlin of malice, though as we shall discover his vengeance when aroused is terrible to behold. And what of the suggestion that Merlin might have been a 'black' magician? It is as well to examine first the kind of thinking that produces such a term. So much nonsense is written about 'diabolism' and 'satanic rites', as if they were legitimate forms of magickal practice, that we must be very wary indeed. 'Evil' may exist as an isolated actuality, but it is doubtful. 'Misplaced energy' might be a better term for anything wholly negative. The modern media thrives on words like *evil*, and in the context of magick, editors perpetuate the equation: magick = drugs, sex, murder. It is in their own interest to do so because such an easy association guarantees sales.

For this reason, magick does not get a good press, even in our own supposedly enlightened times. The innocuous adventures of J. K. Rowling's Harry Potter are regarded as sinister stuff—instruction in diabolism—in some quarters.

This same paranoia extends to the academic world. How many serious writers on the esoteric have discovered that to the publishing fraternity 'shaman' is a better option than 'magician', a book about 'Wicca' rather than 'witchcraft' easier to promote?

The term 'black magic' is meaningless with reference to magick, because magickal energy is always neutral. The *way* it is used determines its character. Even Aleister Crowley, nicknamed by his mother 'The Great Beast', a title which he later adopted for himself, was *per se* no Satanist. He had as much contempt for those who took part in the 'Black Mass' as any magician. Since the 1960s, when all things magickal started to become chic, a desire to emulate the supposed 'image' of Crowley has begun to emerge. Jimmy Page, the rather dull-witted guitarist of Led Zeppelin, even went so far as to purchase Crowley's former home, Boleskine. How can the well-documented twilight zone of rock music and magick make a sensible mix? Dion Fortune advocated a sober and modest lifestyle as being the most suitable for those who were involved with the magickal art, and that advice cannot be bettered.

The magician is truly a person of mystery because his magickal life takes place in the unknown. One could say that everyone's life is mysterious, but the difference is that the majority do not *court* the unknown. Rather, they avoid anything that appears to be ambivalent or disturbing. Paradox, an essential principle of magick, does not sit well with those who embrace a conventional lifestyle. It takes courage to be a magician, and for this reason he is *the warrior* as Carlos Castaneda constantly tells us. The power of the *universe* is of a very different order from the power of *humanity*. It is what keeps the whole thing going, the invisible glue that stops creation from falling apart. *Personal* power is an illusion; there is only *universal* power, which acts through the individual. It is all down to the ego, which is terrified that it will be ignored, and so constantly vies for attention. If it is allowed to dictate *the way we see things,* then it becomes a dangerous tyrant. The ego bullies our perceptions and does not allow anything to intrude into our consciousness that is a threat to its status quo. It insists upon having a monopoly on the truth, but is in fact the source of illusion.

The enemy of the imagination, a positive creative force, is *imaginings.* The monsters in your head need to be slain as quickly as possible, or they will defeat and destroy you. It takes courage to face up to the ego, but once it sees that you mean business it will turn tail and flee. The greatest power that we can access is the Higher Self, which we all possess despite any earthly misdeeds. That is the power that one should refer to, never the ego-self. By jettisoning this burden we gain everything and lose nothing.

* Wunderkind *

Theurgy or high magic is the raising of consciousness to the appreciation of the powers and forces behind the external material world in a pious intention of developing spiritual awareness and subsequently helping to bring to birth the divine plan of a restored earth. Thaumaturgy, or low magic (sometimes called sorcery), is the production of wonders by the use of little known powers of the mind.

—GARETH KNIGHT

Dragons

Merlin was born into a world that had already begun to change radically, particularly in the West. Britain had experienced the arrival and subsequent departure of the Romans, and now the land knew the Age of Kings. The struggle for domination of the kingdom was fought between a few warlords. Into this chaos of alliances, treachery, and bloodshed, Merlin made his appearance—a precocious and visionary youth. He would subsequently leave the world as a sage. In his youth, Merlin has yet another correspondence with the Sun card of the Tarot: here he is the innocent child astride the horse of intelligence. He does not hold onto the horse's mane to save himself, for he is all-trusting. He is also the figure of the Fool, abandoning all earthly constraints and leaping into the unknown, as is always the nature of magick.

He quickly becomes an adviser to a king and a performer of the mystical arts as his subsequent encounter with Vortigern shows. That the tale concerns a red dragon confirms Merlin's affinity with Wales and the deepest parts of the

British psyche. England is ruled by the sign of Aries, the equivalent of the Dragon in the Chinese astrological system.

Merlin's master Vortigern does not enjoy a great reputation in contemporary records. Gildas, the sixth-century historian, will not even admit to him owning any true kingship, describing him as 'a proud usurper'. He is apparently prey also to every conceivable vice. Vortigern is largely remembered for inviting Saxon mercenaries to occupy part of the east coast of England, a move which quickly led to the steady colonization of that part of the country. He is regarded as a dangerous failure, a leader who has suffered from misfortune. From once having control of his Saxon protégés, Vortigern's authority deteriorates completely, and with his court he is forced to flee to Wales for safety.

There, the king seeks to build a mighty tower. When the project is begun the foundations keep sinking into the ground. After consulting his magicians, Vortigern is informed that his project would only be a success if a singular sacrifice is made. The blood of a bastard child must be sprinkled over the foundations. His informants tell Vortigern that the young Merlin would be a suitable candidate. It seems the youthful wizard is as vulnerable as any of the Innocents of Bethlehem. Merlin is sought out and eventually brought before Vortigern. Completely unabashed by his kingly presence, the young wizard quizzes Vortigern about the tower. He castigates the magicians for their lack of insight and provides his own explanation of the problem. Merlin explains that there is a pool of water beneath the tower. At the bottom of this are two hollow stones, one containing a red dragon and the other a white one. When the pool is drained this is found to be so, and the two dragons begin to fight. Merlin explains that the British, represented by the red dragon, will be harried by the Saxons, the white dragon. This situation will continue until the coming of the Sacred Boar, who will defeat them. The 'Boar' that Merlin refers to is, of course, Arthur. Vortigern is so impressed by Merlin's insights that not only does he spare his life, but forthwith gives him a place at court as his personal magician and adviser.

Much insight is to be gained from this episode, our first encounter with the youthful wizard. What is demonstrated is the superior magick that Merlin already has at his disposal. His dismissing of Vortigern's magicians as incompetent charlatans shows that he can be patently right when others are wrong. This is demonstrated again by the account of the soothsayer who travelled to England with the first Saxon fleet and swore to the immediate defeat of the British. That prediction Merlin would also prove to be substantially incorrect.

Alchemical symbolism is present in the tale also. It is not too obscure a task to exchange the lions for dragons and then change white to green. If we do this we have the alchemical process of two organic forces acting to cause change. Merlin will later be associated with the stag, which is another creature that features in the annals of alchemy. No record exists of Merlin being an alchemist, but his superior knowledge of magick would have suggested its fundamental principles. The ability to 'cause changes in consciousness' is at the heart of magick, and this premise may be made clearer if we look further at the art of alchemy and what is involved therein.

This science (Arabic *al-kimia*—the art of transformation) is the father of chemistry. The study began in Egypt and later became established in ancient Greece, India, and China. Its adoption by Islamic culture and its journey to Europe follow the pattern of an osmosis of ideas that prevailed in the Middle Ages. That the goal of alchemy was to transform base metals into silver and gold has passed into common lore. To regard this as the only end is to misinterpret the philosophy behind the alchemist's researches. As Paracelsus wrote in his *Alchemical Catechism*:

Q: When the Philosophers speak of gold and silver, from which they extract their matter, are we to suppose that they refer to the vulgar gold and silver? **A:** By no means; vulgar silver and gold are dead, while those of the Philosophers are full of life.

In its attempt to attain enlightenment, the alchemists' desire to attain the 'Philosophers' Stone' has much affinity with the Grail Quest. The wish to attain the 'elixir of life' and a 'panacea' to cure all ills and prolong life indefinitely was the more practical application of the alchemists' endeavours. It is the more mundane aspect of alchemy that has left its mark. The refining of metals; the invention of gunpowder, ink, dyes, and paints; and their contributions to ceramic and glass manufacture are all the practical result of alchemical investigations.

Earth Energies

Stonehenge is one of the most well-known and celebrated megalithic monuments in the Western world. Even discounting mythical solutions, how it came to be constructed is an age-old mystery. The reason for its being built seems to originate with Ambrosius. Also known as *Ambrosius Aurelius*, he succeeded to the throne on the defeat and death of Vortigern. During the latter's reign, a treacherous plot by Hengist the Saxon had resulted in the massacre of many nobles. It was the wish of Ambrosius to erect a suitable memorial to these fallen warriors. The craftsmen who were summoned by the king seemed strangely reluctant to execute the task, and Ambrosius was obliged to seek out Merlin to ask his advice.

Merlin was adamant that the only monument that would truly do justice to honouring the memory of the fallen was the 'Giant's Dance', a structure of vast stones in Ireland. These stones apparently had the power of healing. Even water that had been first poured over the stones, then used for bathing wounds, had a miraculous curing effect. Ambrosius must have been impressed by Merlin's conviction, as he sent the wizard, accompanied by a small army, to fetch back the stones from Ireland. Merlin achieved this end, naturally aided by his magick, and the stones were set up near the site of the present day town of Amesbury in Wiltshire.

It was discovered a thousand years later that the famous Stonehenge blue stones come from the Prescelly in Wales, and so were transported to their present site. That bare achievement is none the less impressive as it involves conveying the huge *sarsens* over land and also water along the river Severn. It is not so easy to rule out supernatural means in the construction of Stonehenge when considering that extraordinary undertaking. The importance to our wizard of possessing *those particular stones* is significant. Who else but Merlin would fully understand their magickal properties and how they could be used in rituals and otherwise? The stones gave him a powerhouse of energy to work with and all with the support of a monarch. Merlin's close relationship with, even patronage by, kings had begun.

Given that the original purpose of the construction was as a monument to fallen heroes, might not the actual location be of some great significance also? Some scholars propose that Stonehenge was similar to Delphi, making it the Sacred Centre or *Omphalos* of Britain. If the site had oracular powers, combined with the ability to heal, this would explain its continual influence on succeeding generations. Naturally it fell into disuse with the increasing influence of Christianity, but this would be some time in the future. As to the actual chronology of Stonehenge, here history diverges from legend. Work began on constructing Stonehenge in 3100 BCE with the monument falling into disuse around 1100 BCE. As Merlin's activities centre around the sixth century AD, a discrepancy of at least three thousand years seems apparent. Either Stonehenge was constructed in its present location some millennia ago or it was simply moved there using the skills of Merlin. We gain more from regarding the whole episode as an example of a sacred site being preserved by a remarkable magician than attempting to rationalize the historical or geographical aspects.

The tradition that Ambrosius is buried at Stonehenge emphasises the link between kings and megalithic sites. The 'entering of the earth' by the king at the end of his life is a sign of his divine function. The perception of Stonehenge as a 'portal' to another world was understood only too well by Merlin. His own intention may have been to slip away quietly to the other world when he felt that his magickal work upon this plane had been completed. Would his shade have remained as a guardian of the site? The presence of earth spirits and other presences is particularly strong at sacred sites. The vibrations are still potent even though they may have lain dormant for thousands of years.

On a more basic level, the forces of the natural world are ever present in the countryside. To conduct magick in the open air rather than in a temple has an immediacy that suggests Merlin used the world as his temple and then had total command of all the natural forces present. It has to be said that it is not so easy to do magick outside these days, partly because of the possibility that one might be disturbed, and also that the earth's aura is not as powerful as in times past. The magnetic field that surrounds the planet is now probably about half the strength that it was several thousand years ago. For that reason we have to work hard at magick—it does not come as easily as it once did! One is fighting the electronic vibrations everywhere, and they definitely get in the way. The problem is we have come to rely on computers, mobile phones, and the rest of it, and now they most definitely will never go away.

We live in an era that has the mind as its matrix. Our neurons work at full stretch and as I write this, I rely on an electronic device to put my words on a screen and eventually on to paper. Billions of people communicate by radio waves every second. We have built a new world, but we have lost the imagination to build our own temple. To be creative requires mental skills other than reason or logic. The computer can be insidious in the way that it provides endless variations as a substitute for invention. Technology has become so sophisticated that unfortunately many cannot tell the difference between reality and an *image* of that state.

Gateway to the Underworld

Among his many personae, Merlin appears to own the nature of a beast. This apparent conflict between reason and the irrational is part of the inner conflict that rages within his breast. It perhaps fuels his magick, so he becomes a personification of magickal polarity. The notion of a deity or spirit who triumphs over winter and death is embodied in the sacrificial gods such as Osiris, Odin, and even Jesus Christ. Even Father Christmas, wreathed in holly and ivy, has the same air of a woodland spirit who brings life and joy back to the world.

In the English folk tradition the various figures of the Green Man, Jack in the Green, John Barleycorn, and Robin Goodfellow all represent humanity's earthy nature. Robin Hood, the outlaw in Lincoln Green with his Merry Men, is another figure with a mythic status. His partner is Maid Marion, a thinly disguised goddess, probably Aphrodite. Even Peter Pan has an affinity with all this. In the Arabic tradition, *Khidir*, the Green One, is the voice of inspiration, encouraging the artist to work with great devotion. The idea of the artist being inspired by his own creation to attain a finer depiction of his vision is an interesting one. The same image of the foliate head appears in Nepal, India, Tibet, and Mexico; it may have even originated in the East and been brought to the West.

Gwynn ap Nudd or Vindos is the king of the fairies who lives in Annwn—the place of enchantment, the underworld. Associated with both Apollo and Hermes, he thus has regal and magickal correspondences with Merlin. His title 'Lord of the Underworld' echoes the Norse god Odin. He is also Herne the Hunter, but with a greater purpose than merely taking game. His 'ghostly hunt' was recorded in the twelfth century and recorded in the *Anglo-Saxon Chronicle*. Known

as the Wild Hunt, this procession across the sky of head-
less steeds, spectral hounds, known as Yeth, and the souls of
Pagans was to be seen at midnight in winter. Unfortunately
the sight was the harbinger of death and ill fortune. As
Nature began to be tamed by the farming community, the
Wild Hunt was seen less and less, and the only vestige left of
it was the coming of Santa's sleigh on Christmas Eve.

In the English county of Somerset, this parade of the
dead was most likely to be seen at Samhain on November
the first. This ancient festival marks the beginning of the
Celtic year and is thought to be the time when the veil between the worlds is at its thinnest. It was on this night that
the souls of the dead were taken inside Glastonbury Tor.
A portal appeared at the base of the Tor, the entrance to
the Fairy Kingdom. The Teutonic nations regarded Odin
as the leader of the Wild Hunt and referred to the parade
of dead souls as 'Woden's host'. These were considered to
be men slain in battle, thus following the Norse belief in
Valhalla. The tradition appears to be almost as old as war
itself and to have a pedigree perhaps even more ancient
than Woden.

Glastonbury Tor lies at the centre of the isle of Avalon,
the mecca of spirituality in Britain. Crowned by a ruined
tower, all that remains of a church once dedicated to St.
Michael, it is a fascinating sight. The Tor never disappoints
in its ability to create an otherworldly air for those who
venture to its peak. A labyrinthine maze winds around its
conical mass, and an extremely powerful, elemental qual-

ity much like a whirlwind or a vortex can be felt there. The Goddess has her throne here and her dominion over life and death is reflected in the spiral pattern of the Tor maze. The most common association with these forms is as a symbolic depiction of the soul's journey. Dragon energy abounds here as it always does in high places, and some see the Tor personified as a dragon that twists and turns in a space of its own, clear of the surrounding land.

It is, as would be expected, the point where numerous ley lines meet. The 'Michael' and 'Mary' lines cross here, and a maze of energy lines crisscross and envelope the Tor. Other sacred locations on the isle of Avalon—Wearyall Hill, the Chalice Well, and the Abbey—all interconnect with the Tor. Tunnels are said to connect many of these places, indicating that the Tor may have always been a hollow hill.

It has been called a magic mountain, a spiral castle, a Druid College, the Place of the Goddess, and with the most speculation, a landing place for UFOs. Cley Hill, another reputed attraction for alien craft, can be seen from the Tor. Balls of light, of every hue and size, have been seen hovering about the tower. Often these sightings are accompanied by feelings of disorientation as if the observers find themselves floating in the air. Such an otherworldly kingdom would be bound to have associations with the wizard Merlin, and there are many. He is said to be awaiting on the summit of the Tor for the returning Arthur from his Glass Castle. Beneath this great mound are two mighty springs of water, one red and the other white. The similarity to Merlin's encounter in his youth with the two dragons of Vortigern cannot be ignored.

Sacred Kingdom

Arthur would later succeed Ambrosius, and it is after his departure that the Celtic notion of a king being chosen by divine right is born. The notion of kings ruling by the ordinance of some higher power, usually God, is very ancient. The Sumerian king Gilgamesh, who ruled in 2600 BCE, is regarded as the first monarch to possess this almost romantic quality. The tradition persisted, adapted by the Church under the title of the 'two swords', the monarch employing one weapon to defend the faith, the other his realm.

The king was not regarded simply as a ruler or an authority figure. In that society, he represented the cosmic order; he was the deity personified. His fitness to rule depended entirely on his own character, his honesty, his courage and wisdom. The very welfare of his people and the fertility of the land depended entirely on the king. If he failed, then the kingdom fell into chaos. Plagues, failed harvests, and invasion from enemies would result. It is the essential concept of the microcosm and the macrocosm, the belief that in all things dwells the spirit of the Divine.

That the British have recognized monarchical titles for over two millennia is shown by contemporary Roman records which list the leaders of various tribes. The most celebrated were Boudicca, the Queen of the Iceni, and King Caractacus. The latter is, unfortunately for his reputation, remembered mainly for taking refuge in Wales while fleeing from the Roman armies. The later Anglo-Saxon tradition of kingship certainly coloured the view of Chrétien de Troyes, who in the Middle Ages wrote the first tales of King Arthur.

The concept is not always dominated by a male perspective. Rhiannon (*Rigantona*, or Divine Queen), a goddess of great antiquity, would choose as her consort a king. He would then be the guardian of her kingdom. Pwyll, loyal kinsman of Arawn the lord of Annwn, adoringly follows the goddess around the hollow hill which is Glastonbury Tor, and they eventually become lovers. She is known as *Rhiannon of the Birds* and represents the *virgin* in the original sense, which was a woman 'complete within herself'. Rhiannon is also the goddess of sexual love who is free to take any man as her lover. The goddess is energized by sex; she is the Moon to the Sun. In the old English nursery rhyme, Rhiannon is the legendary Lady Godiva who rides naked and unashamed upon her white horse:

Ride a cock-horse to Banbury Cross
To see a fine lady upon a white horse
With rings on her fingers
And bells on her toes,
She shall have music wherever she goes.

Temple maidens once had sacred sex with worshippers, a tradition that, perhaps inevitably, fell into disrepute. Even so, the notion is nonetheless an expression of sex as a Divine Act. The Hindu carvings that so shocked the sensibilities of Victorian explorers were created as a celebration of sex, an outlook that still has its detractors in the West. The Celtic peoples held a view that the sexes were equal and that a woman might choose her partners as freely as any man.

Guinevere is a particular ideal of feminine beauty. *Gwyne-fer* or *Gwen-hwyfar* means 'fair spirit'. Like the Empress of the Tarot, Guinevere has a crown of stars about her—she is Venus/Aphrodite. In another Welsh tradition, she is *Blodwenn*—the 'flower bride' whose physical form is made entirely of flowers. Guinevere is also Queen of the May, her festival being at Beltane on the first day of that month. Guinevere is permanently in white, the badge of her innocence. Her chosen colour may also indicate that she is Etain (Persephone), the underworld bride abducted by Midir. Melwas was the 'King of the Summerland', which refers to the kingdom of the afterlife as well as to the English county of Somerset. His kidnapping of Guinevere, and her being held in Avalon until rescued by Arthur, strongly echoes the aforementioned classical myth.

✶ Birth of a King ✶

There are times in the history of races when the things of the inner life come to the surface and find expression, and from these readings of the veil the light of the sanctuary pours forth.

—DION FORTUNE

Queen of Atlantis

Merlin was closely connected with the Celtic colonizers of Britain, as we shall see. The building of megalithic monuments is entirely attributable to their beliefs and also to their magickal skills. Yet the original inhabitants of Britain were Iberian, the remnants of the advanced civilization that had occupied the island of Atlantis. The old gods before Zeus and the rest of the Greek pantheon were the Titans, and one of these was Titan Albion, the ancient title of the British Isles. The occult tradition of the Titans is often referred to as Atlantean, and much of that magickal lore is embodied in the Round Table and the Holy Grail. The former is a representation of the universe with the sphere of the stars and space. The Babylonian astrologers were as aware of this as their Atlantean counterparts, and their respective lands occupy the same latitude. The tradition that *Druids* originated from Atlantis suggests that the true religion of the world is Druidry, and that Paganism and Christianity are falsifications of that original creed.

Dragons were known in Atlantis, and that is why these fabulous creatures figure so strongly in the tales of Merlin's youth. The pedigree of the wizard as a timeless, universal being is always being re-established. He prefers to be a figure from the unknown, a survivor of a distant civilization. The ways of Atlantis are as mysterious to us as the ethos of ancient Egypt. The supernatural kingdom of Atlantis may too be compared to Avalon—paradise on Earth. At the fall of Atlantis only those who possessed magickal powers escaped the destruction of the island, Merlin being one of the fortunate. Accompanying him was Ygraine, Igraine, or Ygerna, a queen who would continue to maintain her royal status when the two celebrated refugees gained the safety of Britain. This singular female was destined to be the mother of Arthur. In this way she would pass on the sacred blood of the Atlantean priest-kings to him. This bloodline preserved a supreme clairvoyance, a quality that Merlin wished the king of England to possess. This quality, combined with the ancestry of Arthur's future father, will bring about a potent and magickal warrior.

In our consideration of the role of Ygerna, we might consider her three daughters also born in Atlantis—Morgan, Elaine, and Morgawse. Each has a prominent part to play in the Arthurian legend. Morgan is Arthur's true love; Elaine is the mother of Galahad, the only knight to achieve possession of the Grail; and Morgawse is the mother of Gawain. These three figures embody the tri-partite goddess that is to be found so often in the Celtic tradition. Elaine is the virgin or 'devoted daughter'; Morgawse, the bride or mother; and Morgan is the crone or 'femme fatale'. Later they will be the three 'Mourning Queens' who accompany Arthur on his last voyage in the barge that sails to Avalon. The principle of three interrelated elements appears in many guises throughout the Arthurian tales. It is also seen in equally as many diverse forms in the 'Druidic Triad'.

Any account of Atlantis (literally, 'daughter of Atlas') originates from the writings of Plato. He mentions that the country was bequeathed to the god of the seas, Poseidon. The 'Sea Cult' was the worship that preceded the Solar Worship of the Druids. Britain, being an island, naturally embraced such a creed. The power of the sea resides, as would be expected, with the Goddess. Knowing this, Merlin increases his power two-fold by combining the solar and the lunar forces. The Sun power that he has carefully invested in Arthur, along with the Isis force that he nurtures in Morgan le Fay and acknowledges in the Lady of the Lake, reflect the magickal polarity that resides within him. Merlin is god and goddess in an earthly body that immediately becomes celestial when he enters the Inner Planes. For Merlin, magick could manifest in both the inner and the outer worlds. That is why he is reputed to have caused such extraordinary phenomena, such as fireballs and lightning storms.

Plato noted that Atlantis was an island bigger than the whole of Europe and Asia combined. As a political power it was said to have dominated Egypt. Its heritage is preserved in isolated parts of Britain, at sacred sites known for their magickal potency, particularly in South West England, North Wales, and Ireland. This Atlantean atmosphere is at its most powerful in Brittany. Once an island itself, it is culturally isolated even to this day. Ostensibly a Catholic country, there is much that is mysterious and otherworldly there, particularly around the coastal areas of Carnac and St. Malo.

The mode of consciousness that we can attribute to Atlantis is that which we describe as being 'right brain' or intuitive. The Atlanteans were reputed to have the means of communication by means of colour, form, and sound—and thus not limited by any intellectual restraints. Naturally, this approach lends itself to the arts and the practice that is never far away, that of magick. From doomed Atlantis Merlin brought with him to Europe the art of shape-shifting and the power to enter the Otherworld.

Rather than a fruitless search for an actual 'lost continent', regarding Atlantis as a metaphysical idea is the best way to utilise its still-awesome power. It is instructive to reflect upon how Atlantis may be represented as a set of visual images for the purposes of meditation. Merlin, learning his magick in Atlantis, may have incanted spells in the Atlantean language. It is said that the few words that have come down to us possess enormous power. Ygerna too might have been aware, through Merlin, of the power of her inherited language and may have used it to shape events, particularly in her dealings with Arthur and her own daughters. We must not underestimate the power and perception of any queen, particularly one of Atlantis. Both Merlin and Ygerna are the precursors of the Druidic tradition. As has been stated, much Atlantean magic resides in sacred sites, and they are sometimes reputed to be the focus of visitations from UFOs and alien voyagers.

Royal Blood

The Atlantean model of aristocratic priest-kings whose interbreeding ensured that only a particular bloodline succeeded to the monarchy may have predated the same practice common in ancient Egypt. It is reflected in the relationship between Osiris and his sister/wife, Isis. The theocracy of ancient Egypt was intimately involved with the Pharoahs, and heredity depended upon the matrilineal line. The succeeding Pharaoh was always the oldest male heir, and it was incumbent upon him that he marry a female with royal blood. In practice this often meant that Pharaohs married their own sisters or half-sisters. When a Pharaoh died it was important that he leave a female heir, so that she might marry into another dynastic line. Much strategy went into deciding whom to marry so as to continually strengthen the bloodline.

The notion of the divinely chosen ruler is also to be found in several ancient cultures, such as the caste structure of India and the procession of the Dalai Lama in Tibet. In China and East Asia a similar notion called the Mandate of Heaven prevailed. It also sought to establish divine approval for the appointment of the monarch but the Mandate of Heaven was only granted to a just king.

Much speculation surrounds the Annunaki (*those of royal blood*) Sumerian deities, or some say angelic figures. They were assigned by Yahweh, the Hebrew God, to watch over Adam and Eve in the Garden of Eden. This role gave the Annunaki the additional title of 'The Watchers'. Their main purpose seems to have been to ensure the purity of the bloodline from Adam and Eve onwards. As these two were created by God, the theory runs that their offspring would be of divine stock. Unfortunately, the Annunaki rebelled against God and abandoned their mission. This made the DNA of Adam and Eve liable to be eternally defiled. God's solution was to inaugurate the Great Flood and begin the bloodline again, this time with Noah. This plan was only partially successful, as the descendants of Noah were not always averse to marrying outside their racial boundaries. To once more reinstate the purity, Judah—the son of Jacob/Israel—became the first of a royal line intended to continue until the coming of the Messiah. Created concurrently with this dynasty was a line of High Priests that continued through Aaron. Thus the tradition of Priest/King, or the symbiotic relationship between the two ranks, was created many thousands of years before Merlin and Arthur enjoyed this bond.

In the Celtic world, kings and their immediate families were said to be of 'fairy blood', meaning they were the guardians of the royal blood. This can be better understood if we regard members of the elf or fairy kingdom as being the protectors of the earth. They have been known as the 'Shining Ones', a term which can be found in the Egyptian Book of the Dead which speaks of, 'ye shining ones, ye men and gods'. Debate concerning their nature embraces alien giants of great height, angels, and the Elohim, this latter being perhaps the same as the Annunaki. Whatever their origin, the Shining Ones do appear to be somehow allied to the British Isles. It is also said that the Druids were the inheritors of their wisdom and responsible for communicating certain teachings to their people.

The British monarch is still anointed with holy oils and therefore *ordained*. The ceremony is based on that used at the coronation of the Holy Roman Emperor. The symbolism follows the Christian concept of 'royal God-given rights' based on the teachings of the Bible. Proverbs 8:15–16 states, 'By me kings reign, and princes decree justice. By me princes rule . . . ' Romans 13:1 continues the theme: 'Let every soul be subject unto the higher powers. For there is no power but of God: the powers that be are ordained are of God'. The class system in Britain still retains vestiges of this ethos, although those who vie for a republic in the U.K. swear that the country is already unanimously egalitarian. This fantasy can be exploded in an instant simply by observing the ways of Britain. Yet before this argument degenerates into a monarchist lobby, the important point here is that what is ultimately of value can only be an 'aristocracy of the spirit'. This quality is paradoxically democratic. Anyone may ascend to the highest peak of spirituality, as long as they are following the dictates of the Divine Will.

Merlin had sworn a magickal oath promising that the next king of Britain would be a supernatural being. The practical advantage for Merlin was that the king would be sufficiently clairvoyant that he would have direct contact with the Inner Planes. With Merlin to guide him, the king would then follow the dictates of the spiritual guardians of the nation. Relevant here is the notion of the Grail as a 'container', in the sense of *containment* being a synonym of *exclusive*. The *Blood-Royal* was genetically transmitted and conferred kingly characteristics on those who bore even the slightest trace of it.

Supernatural Lord

The political struggle for kingship at this period is quite astonishing in its ruthlessness. What is also extraordinary is the speed at which one monarch succeeds another. Ambrosius and his brother Uther invaded England from Brittany, establishing the undeniable connection which that country has with the Arthurian legends, and inflicted a heavy defeat upon the Saxons. Naturally, this was not a total victory, for the Saxon presence continued to be a threat—one that became so acute that Arthur's campaign against them was the only reason that they did not over-run England as early as the sixth century.

Confronting Vortigern in his stronghold in Wales, Ambrosius and Uther decide to dispatch their enemy by the simple tactic of burning him alive in his own home. Shortly after this violent deed is done, Ambrosius himself meets his end, poisoned by a treacherous Saxon. Uther becomes king and is henceforth known as *Uther Pendragon* (Dragon's Head). Legend has it that a fiery star resembling that creature appeared in the Heavens at the moment of his accession. Uther then engages with the Saxons once more, defeats them yet again, and presides at a victory feast in London.

At this celebration Uther is seized by an overwhelming desire for Ygraine. On two counts is this sudden passion unfortunate. Ygraine is spoken for: she is the wife of Gorlois of Cornwall, and he is one of Uther's most loyal supporters. Gorlois reacts to Uther's blatant attentions by removing himself and Ygraine to Tintagel Castle, where he proceeds to virtually imprison his wife. The thwarted Uther is not best pleased, and intent on finding a solution to this dilemma, summons Merlin. The wizard does indeed have a plan which he proposes to Uther. With the king's approval given, Merlin loses no time in implementing it. Not only does Merlin's scheme suit Uther, it will also fulfill Merlin's oath to bring about the birth of the divine king.

Gorlois is away from his kingdom, leading an attack on Uther's army, and thus leaving Ygraine alone in the castle in Tintagel. Merlin then works some impressive magick upon Uther, using his powers of shapeshifting to good effect for the first time. Uther, having assumed the appearance of

Gorlois, has no difficulty in entering the castle at Tintagel. Assuming she is in the company of her husband, the transformed Uther is invited into Ygraine's bedchamber. That night Arthur is conceived. Born of an Atlantean woman, the future king of England is thus a supernatural being. Gorlois is slain in battle that same night, and Uther marries Ygraine shortly afterwards, almost in indecent haste. Whether or not he ever reveals his deception to his wife is a question never comprehensively answered in the annals.

A similar tale exists in classical mythology when Jupiter sleeps with Alcmene, that union producing Hercules. The common factor in these tales is the ungovernable lust of the male party for the female. No other woman will do; desire must be slaked only with the desired one. It might be said that such a relentless will is akin to the forces of nature. Also it might be speculated that the very nature of the energy evoked unleashes a magickal current that will reside in the offspring. He in turn will demonstrate an occult power to the world. The implications in magickal terms of this birth cannot be underestimated. It might be that Merlin believed Uther Pendragon also had an Atlantean pedigree. The king may have even had remote strains of Lemurian blood in his veins. The civilization of Lemuria predated even Atlantis and was thought to be far more advanced than that country in its refinement of magickal ideas by the priestly caste. Another point in Uther's favour was his being a member of 'Pendragonship'. This exclusive group was a brotherhood of occult warriors whose symbol was a representation of the constellation Draco, the Dragon. In esoteric terms this supernatural creature is to be found at the Northern Pole of the Celestial Sphere, in mundane astronomy the North Star.

Ygraine was one of the Sacred Clan, yet another esoteric group, and unique in that its origins were in both Atlantis and Cornwall. Gorlois' pedigree was nonetheless exotic, for his ancestors were said to be giants from a time before man. Arthur would have absorbed the aura of his father even before his birth, together with the etheric influences from his mother. He would also encounter his half-sister Morgan in a particularly significant meeting, one which would have far-reaching consequences. It is as if Arthur was already steeped in magick even before he entered the world.

Future King

The myth of Arthur, as opposed to what we know of his history, can be compared to that of Heracles, Dionysius, and Beowulf. Myths from distant parts of the world often appear to be similar in structure or content. It seems that the desire to cherish them is a fundamental human need. In any account of a heroic life, the same life pattern emerges. It begins with a strange birth and an upbringing involving a magickal guardian or equally otherworldly foster parents. Danger accompanies his youth always before the time when he will emerge as a man and prove himself by some great deed.

Merlin appears to take the child Arthur under his magickal wing from the very first. He then resides in the castle of Sir Ector or Sir Antor, father of Sir Kay. Both will later be loyal knights of the Round Table when Arthur becomes king. Sir Ector is regarded as the 'foster father' of Arthur, Kay his childhood companion. It is said that Merlin does not reveal Arthur's true destiny to Ector. In an ironic twist, Arthur, being younger than Kay, becomes his squire.

Apart from these incidents, little is known of Arthur's life until he reaches the age of fifteen. He is said to have been a high-spirited, adventurous, and honest lad, in the spirit of his future calling. Arthur's childhood playground is Sir Ector's estate, the Forest Sauvage, which is the setting for later tales involving the Knights of the Round Table when each is upon his individual quest.

As Uther Pendragon lies dying, another victim to Saxon plotting, Merlin makes a prophecy before him. He announces Arthur's succession—the boy will occupy the throne of England that now lies empty. We now begin to see Arthur as a Divine King—as the Messiah, the *Saviour of the Kingdom*. The words of the hymn written by Charles Wesley, the eighteenth-century leader of the Non-Conformist Church in England, lyrically espouses these sentiments:

Hail the Heaven-born Prince of Peace!
Hail the Sun of Righteousness!
Light and Life to all He brings,
Risen with healing in His wings.

William Blake, the poet and visionary, pursued his own singular version of Christianity throughout his life. His visions were inspired by the simple notion that Christ was humanity's link to the Divine. God was in man and thus he too was divine. Blake lived in an era of dualism and embraced that view. The twentieth-century magician would argue that the nature of God is to be both good and evil. God created the world, the world is composed of good and evil—therefore God is good and evil. This simple logic wipes out Christian duality at one blow. Repression, guilt, and denial are the 'virtues' that Christianity has touted for over a millennium as the only means by which a 'sinner' could enter Heaven. This creed, and the advocating of particular behaviour to accompany it, can only be seen for what it is—falsity.

When we evoke the true image of Christ or Buddha, we do not evoke the actual being but a representation of that great power. The act of empowering the unconscious to create the image has the effect of bringing that divine being into the conscious realm. It is the reason why saints and holy persons become the embodiment of their devoted one, as if addressing others with their voice. Merlin is an image of power, one who represents the might of natural forces. His own power resides in the supreme faith that he has in his ability to command these energies. He could not achieve this extraordinary undertaking unless he was totally at one with the forces that he evokes. This means a total abnegation of the personality—he is egoless.

He will be required to prove to the universe, namely his divine masters, that he has achieved this state. He will be forced to do this through enormous sacrifice, as we shall discover. It is important that we understand the real idea behind sacrifice, and the testing of faith that is so intimately bound up with it.

A familiar biblical text tells of the woman who believed that by touching the robe of Christ she would be cured. That is an immense act of faith, engendered by Christ himself. Faith joined with power is divine magick, and doubtless before Christ appeared there were other shamanic-like figures who possessed the ability to ease the physical suffering of their fellows. Osiris was the archetypal sacrificial god—the sacrificial priest and the sacrificial king being variations on the same theme. The legend of the sacrificial king has been cited as the modus operandi of the death of several notable figures in European history. King William II (William Rufus), Archbishop Thomas à Becket, and Joan of Arc may well have been voluntary victims of sacrifice.

Arthur, in the guise of a boar (spring and fertility), slays winter in the personification of Tammuz, the Sumerian deity. As Adonis he is then slain by a boar himself. Shakespeare assigns the wild boar to Richard III, who gores England and brings sterility to the country, turning it into the Waste Land.

In esoteric terms, sacrifice is the direct contact between the Higher Self and the Lower Self. This communication happens very infrequently to the 'ordinary' person, perhaps only when such a person receives some premonition or perhaps during a 'near-death' experience. In the case of a martyr to a cause, whatever that may be, the Higher Self acts upon the Lower Self to such a degree that the latter cannot resist. If suffering and death result, then so be it. The Lower Self may even be unaware of the reasons for the surrendering of its earthly self. The sacrifice, too, may be the result of karma acquired in a previous life, likely to be unknown to the individual unless he or she happens to be very perceptive.

✶ Warrior and Wizard ✶

. . . Magic as black as Merlin could make it, and the whole sea was green fire and white foam with singing mermaids in it. And the Horses of the Hills picked their way from one wave to another by the lightning flashes! That was how it was in the old days!

—RUDYARD KIPLING

King Maker

Uther Pendragon was buried beside his brother at Stonehenge. Two years then elapses before his successor takes
up ruling the kingdom. It was Merlin's task to establish
Arthur, then aged fifteen, as the heir to the throne of England. Merlin invites every member of the British nobility to gather in London at Christmastime. They all duly
appear, well aware of Merlin's purpose in summoning
them—a new king must be appointed. Records mention that the focus of the gathering was to 'observe mass',
which may be an entirely Christianised view of the event.
What is certain is that the entire company, while walking
outside, come upon an anvil or a large stone with a sword
protruding from it. A legend is written in gold upon it:

> Whoso pulleth out this sword of this stone and anvil
> is rightwise King born of all England.

After some encouragement from Merlin, Arthur attempts
this feat and, to the wonder of all, easily removes the sword

from its resting place. He is thus acclaimed king, though not without some opposition from some of the other lords, predominantly one Loth. Some sources report that civil war then ensued; they also note that with Merlin's consummate strategy, all opposition was defeated.

Both the sword and the stone are symbolic artefacts. Arthur was later to be reincarnated as St. Germain, whose consort is Portia, the Goddess of Justice. The sword held by the figure in the Tarot card Justice represents divine truth rather than earthly law. It is significant that Justice is depicted as a female figure, for the feminine force is said not to act but to *react*, and in doing so guards the principle of *equilibrium*. Divine swords feature in various guises in the Bible—held by the cherubim of Eden, Archangel Michael, and the Angel of the Apocalypse. Armed with the sword from the stone, Arthur must experience his first combat. He comes upon King Pellinore in the forest intent on searching out the Questing Beast. This awesome creature, his quarry, has the head and neck of a serpent, the body of a leopard, the haunches of a lion, and the feet of a deer. Its name is not related to the Grail Quest, but comes from its barking cry, 'as thirty couple of hounds *in quest*'—that is, hunting. Arthur attacks his opponent with youthful vigour, but is swiftly trounced and breaks his own sword. Merlin swiftly saves Arthur from further indignities and even death by causing King Pellinore to fall into a deep sleep.

Merlin sets about the task of replacing Arthur's weapon with the aid of the Lady of the Lake, *Vivienne* or *Nimmue*. In a dramatic tableau, her bare arm appears from beneath the surface of the lake holding Excalibur, her gift to Arthur. It is also an offering from Avalon, or more precisely, the spirits in the mists of Avalon, which create in their turn the *Lake of Wonder*. This encounter is a portent for both king and magician, for it will be Merlin's fated encounter with Nimmue that will end his time as adviser to Arthur.

The name *Excalibur* may be derived from the Latin phrase *Ex calce liberatus*, 'liberated from the stone', which might imply that the sword in the stone and Excalibur are one. This apparent confusion disappears when we consider the custom in Celtic times for leadership disputes to be resolved by single combat in the centre of a stone circle. The victor 'drew' or took 'a sword of office' from a stone altar, thus the term *sword in stone* was derived in this way. The tradition of the king being chosen at an assembly within a stone circle persisted into the time of the Saxon kings. Ethelbert (860–65) was crowned at Kingston-upon-Thames (Kings' Stone), as were his father and brother.

The name may also derive from either the Old French *Escalibor Caliburn* or the Latin *Caliburnus* or *Chalybs*, meaning 'steel'. In the Tales of the Mabinogion the sword is known as *Caledvwlch* or *Caldbolg*, meaning 'hard belly—consuming anything'. A close derivation is *Caladfwlch* or *Calad-bolg*—'hard lightning'. We are reminded of Jupiter, depicted with three thunderbolts, chance, destiny, and providence. The king of the gods is associated with fire as is another god, Vulcan, constantly working at his forge. Excalibur is said to have originally been borne by the Irish hero Cu Chulainn. Malory in Le Morte d'Arthur has given us two evocative descriptions of the celebrated sword: in battle, 'Fire springs from the serpents upon the hilt', and Arthur wielding the weapon '. . . so bright in his enemies eyes it gave light like thirty torches'.

Arthur is said to be the true owner of Excalibur, because it is a 'Sun weapon' and Arthur is a Sun god as we have learned. The magickal sword has 'Take me' in runic script on one side of the blade and 'Cast me away' on the other. At the death of Arthur, the knight Bedivere is given the task of returning the sword to the lake. It takes him three attempts to do this; on the first two occasions he cannot bring himself to cast away such a beautiful object. At last he succeeds, and as the sword flies gratefully out across the water, the hand of the Lady of the Lake grasps Excalibur once more and disappears below the waters for the last time. The tradition of making offerings of weapons to the river god Silvanus may have prompted such an aspect in the tale.

Tennyson, the Victorian poet, describes Excalibur as having

> . . . the haft twinkled with diamond sparks,
> Myriads of topaz lights, and jacinth work . . . [2]

---

2. In "Morte d'Arthur" (1838).

Any medieval description of the sword would have made reference to the skills of contemporary swordsmiths. Their employing of gold and jewels when decorating the hilt and pommel of a sword was masterful. Perhaps Wayland, the celebrated smith of Albion, forged Excalibur? His spirit lives on in the long barrow named Wayland's Smithy, near Uffington, Oxfordshire, in the heart of the dragon landscape. Smiths, like magicians, were autonomous figures, their status so high that kings would request their services. The magician's sword is an essential part of his magickal armoury. The design of a *magickal sword* provides the clue, for its hilt must be of copper, the metal governed by Venus, the beneficent planet, so that it balances the iron of Mars. This is a meeting of God and Goddess, and without such a union the sword is worthless as a magickal artefact.

Merlin is the most celebrated magician in the Western Magical Tradition. The closeness of his relationship with King Arthur suggests that they could together make a composite figure—the magician being the inner self and the king the outer manifestation. Merlin is the Knowledge, Arthur the Will—the essential principles for any magickal practice. It is an *equal* relationship, for as we have seen, Merlin is not in thrall to kings; he is his own man. The actor, as does the jester, abandons his own personality for the sake of his art. He chooses the persona he wishes to assume and wholeheartedly becomes that character. To set aside the ego is the ultimate liberation for the spirit.

The Eastern tradition has always maintained that enlightenment can only begin with the end of the self. Merlin's magickal powers enable him to transcend the ego and become anything he wishes. Could such a man ever take seriously the fripperies and foolishness of a court?

Round Table

The Round Table was owned by Leodegrance, the father of Guinevere. When she is wed to Arthur, Merlin suggests that it becomes part of her dowry. The circle is a female symbol, and the power of Guinevere, who personifies the earthly form of the kingdom, is contained within it. The company of knights begins to assemble as soon as the Round Table makes an appearance. This is the moment when its power begins to be evident. We have already encountered the Celtic tradition of choosing a king from a company assembled at a sacred site. The Round Table is an idealistic form of a stone circle. The *purpose* of such megalithic monuments has been researched by this writer for some time. That their design reflects the pattern of the Heavens seems more than likely. It would follow that Merlin's eagerness to acquire the Round Table is an indication that he regards it as a macrocosm of the galaxies. Merlin's obsession with stargazing and all it entails will grow more intense, as we shall discover.

The Round Table may also be an evocation of the table of the Last Supper. In this guise it becomes the 'Grail Table' and is a microcosm of perfection. It might also be thought of as a symbol of the 'perfect world', part of the Rules of Chivalry. Yet it is not mathematically perfect. Twelve places are assigned and one remains empty—the 'Siege Perilous'. The seat is assigned to the 'Grail Hero', the only knight to fulfill the Quest. The thirteenth place should not be occupied by a human, because that is the rightful place of God. It was also on the thirteenth day of his life that the Magi came to visit Christ, hence the magickal association with that number. Thirteen is also the sum of the first two squares, four and nine. And what is the significance of the number twelve, a natural harmonic, or, more importantly, of thirteen? Sacred kingship requires a ruler to personify the solar deity. Apollo/Odin/Arthur, or whoever may be considered, is served by twelve lesser god-kings, corresponding to the twelve zodiacal signs which structure and govern the cosmos. This ancient idea can be taken further to suggest that the country is divided by radial lines from its centre into twelve separate sections. According to this theory, each has not only its own astrological attributes, but an association with a note in the twelve-tone scale.

Naturally the *number* of places at the table is significant—thirteen—the total of the lunar months. Several examples of fellowships of men with this number—those of Sanat, Kumara, Buddha, Confucius, and Quetzalcoatl—have existed at different times. These 'various mythological companies' have always consisted of a leader and twelve followers. Christ and his twelve disciples is the most obvious example, as Odysseus and the Twelve and now Arthur and his Knights. Can the Round Table be the wheel of the zodiac, with each knight given an astrological sign? A correspondence might also be found with the Tarot. We might consider the first twelve cards of the Major Arcana from the Fool (o) to the Hanged Man (XI). The tradition that thirteen is unlucky originates with Judas Iscariot, the betrayer of Christ, being the thirteenth disciple.

The knights who occupy the places at the Round Table are without exception aristocrats. They are all the wealthy sons of the gentry, each with his own squire. It is telling that in the Tales the giants with whom the knights are constantly called to fight are brutal and mindless. More than a hint exists that the hero is, *fait accompli*, a member of the nobility. The giants always remain as commoners. Like Robin Hood's companions, many of the knights are household names. Of them, Lancelot (du Lac or del Acqs), is the most celebrated, mainly because he is the lover of Guinevere. This classic ménage à trois is rivaled only by the Comedia dell'Arte trio of Harlequin, Columbine, and Pierrot.

Galahad is the son of Lancelot, and in an echo of the manner of Arthur's birth does his conceiving take place. Lancelot is visiting the Castle Carbonek in his Quest for the Grail. While he is there a young woman falls instantly in love with him. She is Elaine, a Grail Bearer and also the daughter of Pelles. While confessing her passion to another of the Grail Maidens, a plan is made. It is one almost identical to the tale of sorcery that accompanies the birth of Arthur. By magickal means her companion makes Elaine seem to assume the appearance of Guinevere. Unaware that the woman in his bed-chamber is not his true love, Lancelot sleeps with her. The fruit of their union is a son, Galahad, the only knight who succeeds in possessing the Grail. The question of how Galahad, born out of wedlock, can be considered pure enough to posses the Grail looms large. It is reconciled by the fact of Elaine being a virgin before her union with Lancelot, which is apparently enough reason for her son to claim the requisite purity. Medieval morality is certainly ambivalent!

Merlin's World

The degree of influence that Merlin has upon Arthur's life cannot be underestimated. Yet Merlin comes and goes from the company of his monarch as he pleases, and it would not be any other way. Thus Merlin's life is lived on many different levels, and it is sometimes not easy for any biographer to untangle the various threads of his existence. If one accepts that this diversity is Merlin's nature, then any account of him is bound to resemble a kaleidoscope of impressions. The only constant in his life is the practice of magick, and this must be the starting point for any understanding of not only his powers, but also the potential of those powers. When we attempt to describe the nature of magick, we are really attempting an explanation of how the universe works. Any debate must include speculation as to what *existed before existence*. Of this, Lao Tzu has this to say in the *Tao Te Ching*:

There is a thing inherent and natural,
Which existed before heaven and earth,
Motionless and fathomless,
It stands alone and never changes;
It pervades everywhere and never becomes exhausted.
It may be regarded as the Mother of the Universe,
I do not know its name.[3]

Merlin is able to travel freely through space and time. He knows even the time before the dawn of creation. Every magician, when he is conducting a ritual, creates a 'space of working', a physical area that is isolated from the 'real world'. A temple is created specifically for this purpose, but magick may indeed be performed anywhere. This 'sacred space' is not dependent upon the laws of physics as they are generally understood. What the magician achieves, or seeks to achieve, during his ritual depends upon his experience and personal ability. All of us have limitations, mostly of the imagination, but all is possible. Magick is an eternal power existing beyond all consciousness. It is dependent on nothing and yet employs every single atom as its medium.

So, for one with Merlin's aptitude, *creating the world* is not impossible. And if he has done this feat once, why should he not do it again? Consider, when he stands atop the mountains with his staff, is it not a simple task for him to control the elements of the weather? Merlin's Pan-like

---

3. Lao Tzu, *Tao Te Ching*, trans. by Ch'u Ta-Kao. (London: Allen & Unwin, 1937).

nature enables him to draw on the energy of the Earth. He combines this force with the other three elements— Water is the Goddess of the Lake, the Wind is purifying thought. The wizard requires a special form of Fire: lightning, the symbol of inspiration. Now he is master of all the world. Merlin stands with Thoth as one of those who works 'behind the scenes' to order the universe. He is an instrument of the Divine Power—in an allegory with the Egyptian scheme, the 'voice of Ra'. Witness his ordering of events in Arthur's reign; Merlin is one who promotes the ways of the Otherworld upon this plane. Mighty indeed is his role in the order of things, and no other magician ever came close to owning and sustaining such power.

The magicians of the early twentieth century were aware of the powers latent within the unconscious. They believed that there was preserved a record of every experience undergone by the individual. Whether they were aware of such memories did not matter. Astral experiences and recollections of past incarnations were also stored in the unconscious. Concurrently with these magickal schools, Jung had this same realization. Such agreement from one of such stature in the relatively new field of psychology gave a fillip to magicians such as Dion Fortune. Merlin, though he would not have voiced it, would have used this mind energy as fuel for his magickal endeavours. For nothing distracts the magician from his purpose. He treats his calling with the utmost seriousness, yet he does not take *himself* seriously. During the journey of purification that all magicians must undergo, the magician loses any sense of 'self'. He realises he no longer requires a 'personality', as his *magickal persona* will suffice. The magician has no interest in artifice or ambition. Adhering to illusions, a practice to which we are very prone in the West, is the result of *bad magic*.

Passions are also anathema to the magician. 'Passion is the enemy of wit' is a sound maxim. To be angry with another person implies that somehow their actions are of some importance. The magician knows that the doings of human beings are never of the slightest consequence. Merlin, although he is a supreme protector of the earthly plane, is indifferent to its fate. That is not to say that Merlin does not love the world—he succours and protects it. But his is a stern love, and he allows nothing to cloud his judgment or foil his intent. We have only the barest details of Merlin's relationships. It seems that his only intimacy is with his wife *Guendolena*, the Flower Maiden. Very little is recorded about her and even less about her life with Merlin. We shall gain some insight into her character later in the story, and in dramatic circumstances. Some have tried to link Merlin with the female guide *Elen of the Ways*, a female version of Mercury, the guide of travellers, but this is probably a confused interpretation of the god's hermaphrodite nature. Both male and female elements are within Merlin and Elen, but they are not two separate figures who wish to be joined. Theirs is not the relationship of Cupid and Psyche.

Merlin appears to have sexual relations with Guendolena on the astral plane as well as in the physical realm.

Merlin later rejects her, but we assume this to be an indication that his path has led away from earthly pleasures and is now exclusively spiritual. With reference to the Qabalah, Merlin is now ascending the Middle Pillar to Kether (The Crown), the influence of the Divine upon the material plane. When he becomes a seer, Merlin achieves the title of this Sephira—'The Ancient One' or 'The Ancient of Ancients'. Linked with all this: the first Hexagram of the I *Ching* is 'The Creative', or 'The Source of All'. It is the fate of Merlin to be involved in the ways of humanity, for as an enlightened being, all natures are within him, though he is wearied by such knowledge. Like the sacrificial priest who seeks through his death to enlighten those he serves, Merlin forever encourages people to be part of the natural world, knowing that will be the way to his salvation.

A Celtic Vision

The name *Wales* derives from the proto-Germanic word *Walha*, meaning 'foreigner' or 'stranger'. King Arthur seems to be exclusively an English hero and although he may have been *Artorius* to the Romans, the name *Arthur* seems intrinsically English. Glastonbury and the Kingdom of Avalon is the stage for the Arthurian tales, of that I am certain. Equally, the landscape of Merlin is firmly set in Wales. Some scholars argue for Caledonia in Scotland as the setting for Merlin's endeavours, but the argument is not convincing. The claim for a *Welsh* Arthur appears around the time of Henry II, inspired by a desire for a

Welsh hero to stand against the monarchy. It has taken
one of our foremost academic historians, Professor Ronald
Hutton in his *Witches, Druids and King Arthur*, to untangle
the two separate traditions. *Carmarthen* has an etymological link with Merlin, and Craig-y-Ddinas in Glamorgan is
known as Merlin's cave. Dinas Emrys in North Wales is
Merlin's stronghold. Of all the Welsh locations associated
with Merlin, to me Llyn y Fan Fawr is the most evocative.
I can only offer an account of my own pilgrimage to this
place of wonder and the visions that I experienced there.

Set within green luminous heights, the preserve only
of sheep and cattle, this Paleolithic lake has more than an
air of mystery about it. Roman legionnaires cannot have
been enthusiastic at the prospect of a posting here; it is a
land meant only for the hardy. The way is still determined
by the ancient sheep tracks, twisting and winding about
the hills. Once there, it is a steep climb to the lake, with
an interval to inspect the fishery where the salmon of wisdom leap into the air, perhaps trying to escape from their
watery enclosure. Although describing another part of
Great Britain, a phrase of the poet A. E. Housman—'blue
remembered hills'—came to mind as I looked back to inspect the view now stretching endlessly into the distance.
Colours were so very vivid on that bright August after-
noon. The sheer cliffs towered above the lake all in emerald
green, but slit in places to reveal red earth, the colour of a
vamp's red lips. A rushing stream accompanied the path to
the lake, its music eventually fading and the sound of one's

breathing all that could be heard, along with a caressing wind and the odd sheep cry. I realized that my companion had no desire for words, and neither did I. In silence we blessed the occasion, and were blessed in return by this wondrous place.

My first sight of the lake was astonishing, because the picture I had envisaged of the place was almost identical to how it now appeared before me. The scene was set, even down to the steady rippling water and the shadows of the still patches near to the banks. The cliff opposite was shaded, too, and stretching nearly to the water's edge, making a dark contrast to the glittering blue-grey of the lake. The diamond flashes on its surface bestowed a continual life and animation on the water. Mesmerized at first by the sight, I began gradually to be aware of a line stretching from bank to bank in the centre of the lake. This division created a strange perspective in two distinct levels. It marked where the Lady of the Lake had her kingdom! No sooner did that realization come to me than I heard a splash of oars. I did not need to gaze too long at the two figures in the boat to know their identity. The craft began to glide slowly but determinedly out from the bank. The drama would unfold on centre stage!

A few more strokes of the oars and the pale, slim arm rose from beneath the lake. Almost soundlessly Excalibur was raised aloft. The sun kissed the jewels on the haft of that sword of sorcery. In a moment the bows of the boat drew nearer, and the king leaned forward to grasp his priceless gift. The grip of the lady loosed and I saw the fingers of the hand open, pale and splayed in a momentary gesture of farewell. That beautiful limb returned silently beneath the shining surface of the lake, with the automatic grace of any creature whose home is water. At that moment two hawks hovered high above, a reminder of the element of Air, symbolic of the sword—the keen edge of clarity. The boat returned to shore, the ravens following in its wake. The Magician, his cloak wrapped about him and in deep thought, the King gazing in wonder at his prize. I realized the scene was not part of this late summer day; this was another season—spring, when entirely new fortunes are born. The time after Imbolc when the Goddess reigns.

This vision gone, I was given another, as butterflies flitted in the sun about me. The lake was the womb and from it flowed life—endless, rippling, moving ever onwards. We join with this tide when we are born, drawn along for a time until we take our leave; but always the waters continue. Ever have they done so and ever they will do. The words of a school hymn came unbidden into my mind: 'Time like an ever-rolling stream bears all its sons away'. My companion and I gathered a stone or two as a memento; then we returned along the path, now talking together freely. We exchanged remarks with the same eagerness that we had felt earlier to be silent. Our surroundings had determined how we should be. That is the power of a sacred landscape.

A coda to the experience was added when I was told the story of the cairn that stood atop of one of the peaks overlooking the lake. Excavations had discovered the bones of a woman and a child within. She must have been a figure of some great importance to have merited such a grand interment. The site of the cairn is in an inaccessible place, and the intense labour that would have been needed to create such a memorial is hard to imagine. Great was the dedication of our ancestors! Most touching of all, in a gesture presumably made by her grieving partner, was that the woman and her child had been laid tenderly upon sheaves of meadowsweet flowers. A fitting farewell for a queen and a princess, or perhaps just those who were once greatly loved.

∗ Divine Madness ∗

*Why do you ask me about death when you do not know
how to live?*

—CONFUCIUS

Death and Change

A total change in consciousness may be caused by any of a myriad of states—love, danger, illness, tragedy, drugs, or visions. Whatever the catalyst, the result is to experience a totally different view of the world. For Merlin, death was the prompt and with it came a fearful madness. Our modern age would refer to 'post-combat stress', and certainly the effects of war must go deep into the psyche. Any conflict fought in the Dark Ages would have been a bloody affair and not easily forgotten except by the most battle-hardened veteran. Debate continues as to the precise location of the relevant battle and even the identity of the enemy. Did Merlin fight alongside Rodarcus, King of the Cumbri, against Guennolous, the King of Scotia (Scotland)? If he did, in this conflict three brothers of whom Merlin was very fond perished in the battle. Alternatively, the death of Gwenddolau, his friend and mentor, slain by the Saxons at the battle of Arderydd, might have brought about his insanity.

If the latter account is correct, the historian will imply that the Celtic culture is dying with Gwenddolau, and has its swan song in Merlin. Rhydderch Hael, the victor, is a Christian king, and Merlin fears he and his men will persecute the wizard because of his beliefs. In some accounts Merlin becomes king and rules Gwenddolau's kingdom for a time. It is also suggested that he was once king of the Demetae, the men of Dyfed in southwestern Wales.

Whether one or both accounts are merely allegories of Merlin's endless powers—the Wizard as King—is not clear. The outcome, however, is the same. Merlin flees into the forest and wanders among the trees in a hopeless delirium. What were the feelings he experienced? Although a wizard, he was still a mortal man. We can speculate that despair, anger, and a strange vulnerability were among his emotions. All this perhaps was greater than any anxiety about losing his sanity.

The concept of 'normality' is relatively modern—eccentricity of behaviour being once a hallmark of the English character. Visionaries, hermits, and saints would have been less of a rarity in Merlin's time, so his behaviour would not have been judged with reference to any rigid standard of conformity. In the twenty-first century, society is all too ready to decide what is 'appropriate behaviour'. The result has been legislation against the medium and the clairvoyant. Our obsession with quantifying everything has become detrimental to our spiritual well-being.

Merlin must weather the psychic storm until he gains the wisdom that will enable him to attain the next level of his enlightenment. He must endure in order to gain, for this is not his end but his beginning. Those on the threshold of spiritual transformation often experience a 'paradoxical disequilibrium'. Merlin has become unbalanced, and he must regain his position on the Middle Pillar of the Qabalah Tree of Life. Every trained magician is familiar with the old adage, 'To Know, to Will, to Dare, and to Be Silent'. He learns which approach of these four to employ at any particular moment. Only with this skill does he remain in harmony with the universe. When an occultist as powerful as Merlin is out of kilter, the result is a full-blown disorientation. His power, volatile because it is a combination of the elements of Fire and Air, implodes and shatters his reason.

Fear gives rise to imaginings—the distorted detritus of the mind. Only when the mind is calm are true visions seen. This is the Darkness of Initiation, and not even Merlin can escape this 'harrowing of hell'. It is an essential part of the magickal journey to encounter great danger, when the mettle is tested and the core is shaken. It is at these moments that the soul comes into its own, soaring to heights unimaginable. The intensity of the experience creates the energy to deal with the disturbance. It is as if the balance must always be maintained—the greater the crisis, the more rewarding the subsequent gain. Within one's own mind dwell the most hideous monsters created by oneself. They are composed of fears, unfulfilled desires, and probably karmic debts. Their purpose is to obstruct the spiritual development and to dissuade the initiate from remaining on his path. The truly enlightened person has had to learn to deal with this challenge, and he knows his magickal education would be incomplete without it. It is admittedly a terrifying and debilitating experience, and there is little consolation in being informed that the higher one ascends the spiritual mountain, the bigger the demons that are lying in wait there.

It is love that scatters these shadows, making them scurry back to the dark corners where they belong. If fear is our most negative emotion, then love is the most positive. With love there is nothing in this world that cannot be achieved. Love of one's self is an essential step before one can love another, then ultimately *universal love* should follow. Merlin's madness can be seen as another step on the way to becoming the ultimate *seer*. His is the most significant sacrifice since Osiris was mutilated by his brother Seth. Merlin's destruction and resurrection is a manifestation of yet another magickal paradox. Two apparently irreconcilable principles—chaos and light—meet to create a third element—understanding. A state of equilibrium returns when Merlin finds succour through the healing element of Water. Only then does his reason return.

Merlin is the first magician to embrace male *and* female energies. His alter egos, Morgan le Fay the sorceress and Nimmue the water nymph, both act as his shadow, throwing into relief his own magickal character. His relationship with them both is the foundation for the alchemical symbiosis of the Sun and the Moon. Thus Merlin establishes a magickal template for the magicians of the Renaissance to follow. His love for Nimmue, which effectively ends his association with Arthur, is far more than the folly of an old man. It is the necessary transformation of the old star magick into the era of the wise woman.

Wild Wizard

Study again the Magician of the Tarot, he is *alone*. The card of the Hermit, the dark side of Mercury, makes the point even more tellingly. The magickal calling is not conducive to society and the social whirl. Sharing experience is a definite need for most *Homo sapiens*; they seek to refer to each other, but magicians as a rule do not yearn for the company of others. For Merlin his situation was even more extreme, and he found himself lonely and isolated. Perhaps his state was even more acute for he knew he could gain no solace from the love or friendship of any mortal. Even the deities seemed to have deserted him. Where was Lugh? Where was Rhiannon? As Merlin was as close to being a god himself as it is possible for any mortal to be, perhaps he felt that any plea would have been as him making exhortations to a mirror. He could only hope that the Heavens might at some time in the future prefer a whole wizard to a demented version.

As has been said, the only demons are those that we invoke in the mind. Our mistakes and unfulfilled desires accumulate in a part of our psyche that astrologers designate to be the Twelfth House. Once called the House of Undoing, it is ruled by Neptune, the planet of delusion. None can aid Merlin as he wanders delirious in the wild woods, neither would they be able to gaze on his tortured countenance, nor listen to the ravings that pour from a soul in agony. For Merlin the experience is literally mind-blowing, and his heart yearns for that most precious of all states—peace of mind. The magickal energies have polarized and are temporarily impossible to reconcile. Visions follow one another with mind-warping intensity. His fevered mind has given him an extraordinary perception so that he can observe the secrets of all things. But the price of such revelations is too high.

Eventually the momentous force produced by his mental conflict will give rise to a third element. This god-energy, being superior to the man-made invention of duality, will eventually bring clarity to him. Not that this knowledge can make the tortures Merlin has to bear any less debilitating and painful. But he is a man of fortitude, who would agree with the sentiment of Winston Churchill: 'When you're going through Hell, keep on going'. Merlin has no desire to be mad, nor does he enjoy his madness. It is just brain fever, and although it brings insights, in his heart he knows they have no value per se. A few of our more vociferous New Age visionaries might learn from this as they broadcast disordered revelations to the world while believing them to be divine messages.

As one who debates the subject of magick, I am often called upon to explain its nature. For the intuitive, it is easier to comprehend metaphysics than physics. Science has never found a role for the imagination, actively shunning this quality of the mind since the eighteenth century. Understanding the idea of the 'Magickal Imagination' is an essential part of any definition of magick. In doing so, one should be careful to distinguish between 'fantasy' and 'imagination', as they are most certainly not the same thing.

Magick schools teach that the imagination may be trained to create an Inner World, so 'real' that it may be summoned and entered at any time. The purpose of this exercise is to gain access to the Inner Planes—the timeless dimension where the magician experiences, and participates in, events beyond ordinary consciousness. A *fantasy* is a conscious desire to picture a world that is 'extra-ordinary', a willingness to take part in a daydream or a 'pipe dream'. Its purpose is to divert or entertain the self or others. A writer of fantasy, such as Terry Pratchett, masterfully achieves this end. It is interesting that Pratchett often satirises all things esoteric, and in interviews has been actively dismissive of anything 'spiritual', or 'New Age'. In doing so, Pratchett aligns himself with the godless scientist, which is perhaps his intention.

None may affect the destiny of the magician; they do not possess the power to effect any change. He is beholden only to the gods of magick, whoever or whatsoever he deems these to be. The magician is master of his destiny, and Merlin, being the greatest of the magi, not only wills what is to happen, but divines the outcome. Lesser magicians fall foul of the errors and temptations that can beset any mortal. The great crises of life help to shape us and make us what we really are. The mettle of Merlin had been tested, and he realises he has only one course left—that is, to leave his fate in the hands of Spirit. In doing so, he forever demonstrates his utter faith and affinity with the workings of the cosmos. Having served the Earth Mother so well in providing a god king who would serve and protect her, Merlin requests the Goddess to sustain his own being in this time of trial.

Shaman

All times of trial have but one result for those of us upon the magickal path—that of discovering who we are. It is also a question of 'who we might be', for none of us, until we encounter such a test, can know how we will react. As nothing remains constant so we will be tested again and again, even as our understanding grows. Merlin does not make mistakes; he accepts any situation for what it is and acts according to his instincts. The term *instinctive* is apposite, because it is how animals react and much of the shamanic tradition includes animals as totem spirits. We shall now investigate shamanism as part of our study.

The tradition originates in Siberia and Mongolia, and *shaman* means 'one who knows'. That 'knowing' is of the folklore, and thus the mindset, of the people whom the shaman aids. For them he provides explanations of the changes in the world, and he achieves this by entering the supernatural world and encountering the spirits that reside there. His interaction with these beings enables him to find ways to treat illness, or to gain answers to questions. He travels in two spheres—the 'upper world' associated with, among other images, mountains and the sky, and the 'lower world' with caves and tunnels.

The initiation of a shaman is often brought about by serious illness or even a near-death experience. Here we see a parallel with the 'initiation' of Merlin through his madness. The shaman also has an 'initiatory crisis' when he acts in a disturbed or bizarre manner, and Merlin has this experience as well. The shamanic practice of 'shape-shifting' is intrinsic to Celtic lore, and Merlin has been a dwarf, a damsel, a page, a greyhound, and an owl. His totemic creatures include the stag, pig, wolf, and goat. But before we are tempted to label Merlin as the 'first of the shamans' we should note a basic difference in approach between the two traditions. This is in the understanding and purpose of the soul. In Celtic animism, all things in the world are considered to possess a soul, thus they are linked in a universal whole. In the shamanic tradition *souls* are seen as separate entities, to be contacted, controlled, or released as the shaman sees fit. Meeting with these souls is achieved by various means, generally through ecstatic trance.

It seems evident that Merlin is not in the business of evoking spirits for the purpose of solving personal problems. In his magickal practice he employs natural energies to cause changes in the material world, but this is not the same as the 'shamanic journey'. Many magicians regard the *evoking* of spirits as a dangerous, even pointless, exercise. *Invoking* Qabalistic or angelic essences is a very different procedure. It is one that is favoured by magicians, and more often than not provides the desired result. There are 'dabblers' who are foolish enough to attempt to evoke spirits from the lower astral planes. If they are successful, and fortunately for themselves they rarely are, they may have to deal with something very nasty indeed. Certainly the shaman and the wizard share common beliefs, and both are prepared to voluntarily involve themselves in uncanny experiences. The magician espouses a state of complete freedom, independent of his earthly existence. The shaman goes even further, embracing the idea that his greatest achievement would be to attain a state of permanent death. If he is aware that he is dead then he has nothing to fear. Thus, his perceptions may be tempered by a constant awareness of the presence of death, leading to a truer perspective of life.

Jung speaks of the 'Shadow', that darkness that we all possess and that is part of ourselves whether we wish it to be or not. It is lodged in the unconscious and owes its form to the material that is at odds with the consciousness of its owner. Its nature is primitive and as yet not integrated in the whole being. The Shadow occupies that path on the Qabalah Tree of Life between Malkuth and Yesod. It must not be regarded as being the same as the 'Dweller on the Threshold'. The only link between the two is in the realm of past lives. The Shadow is only attached to the individual's present incarnation. The Dweller on the Threshold combines all the past lives of the individual and is in the Eastern view the 'facing up' to personal karma. Upon the Qabalistic Tree it would correspond to the sphere of Chesed. To continue with the Qabalistic correspondence, an *integration* of the soul is achieved in the sphere of Tiphareth, but this is not enough to sever the ties of the past. It takes a journey across the abyss of Daath to wholly achieve this. In appearance, the Dweller is terrible to behold, a reversal of the Higher Self, yet only the part that has not yet been integrated. Thus a divine quality surrounds it.

Merlin is only too aware of this figure that inevitably he must face, and he also knows that his personal suffering will go some way to ridding himself of any karmic debts.

Wild Beast

The Chinese regard the dragon as a celestial stag, and this magnificent creature is a prominent symbol in many cultures. A *white stag* is often sent as a guide by the denizens of the Otherworld. It also may be the lord of that place. A proud and highly aware animal, it represents the power of the mind. It is a symbol of alertness and a readiness to follow the intuition of dreams, thus acknowledging transformation. In the Middle Ages, the devices painted on shields were designed to give protection in battle. The stag is ubiquitous in heraldic designs because of its supposed mystical power. Among the ancients, the priest-god adorned himself with stag's horns to identify with his quarry, hunter and hunted then becoming one.

The most renowned deity of the hunt is Diana. Artemis, the sister of Apollo, is also a goddess of the hunt and the Moon, as Diana. In the link with Apollo the alchemical joining of the Sun and Moon is symbolized. The god who personifies both the hunter and the hunted is Cernunnos (Gaulish—*carnon*—antler; Old Irish—*cern*—horn). He is 'Lord of the Animals' who has through the ages come down to us as Herne the Hunter. Similar deities exist in other cultures: Pan of the Greeks, the Minotaur of the Minoans and Pashupati, the Hindu 'Lord of the Animals'. These three entities may have had a common myth to unite them, but if so it still lays undiscovered. Cernunnos was also not above regarding his enemies as his prey and hunting them down as well. Let us observe how Merlin, too, is capable of one deadly act of vengeance.

A bizarre sequence of events leads to an equally strange tragedy. Still in the grip of madness, Merlin returns briefly to the court where his wife Guendolena still pines for him. She tells Merlin that she will willingly live in the forest with him. Merlin is callously indifferent to this declaration of loyalty and love. On Guendolena enquiring if she should remain a widow or marry again, Merlin gives his permission for her to be wed. This apparently selfless gesture is tainted by Merlin's warning that if he encounters the bridegroom before the wedding, death will be his lot. In the tale Merlin then assures Guendolena that he will attend the nuptials and bestow great gifts upon her. We are not entirely convinced by these sentiments. A sinister air hangs upon his words, and we are right to be wary.

Merlin duly appears at the wedding ceremony riding upon a stag. A procession of these animals as well as goats wind along behind him. On his arrival at the castle, a man laughs at him from a high window. Merlin, recognising the future husband of Guendolena, kills him with great violence. Merlin flees towards the haven of the woods, but the river prevents his escape and he falls into the water. The juxtaposition of the stag as the symbol of fire energy and the water energy of the river is significant. The glyph of fire is a triangle, that of water the triangle inverted. Put together they form the Seal of Solomon, otherwise known as the Star of David. This powerful magickal symbol implies completion and a state of rest. It also bestows protection upon the wearer. It is as if Merlin has reached yet another stage of initiation and waits for its culmination. He is still prey to the wildest of emotions—the rage of the beast—but this will prove a turning point in the saga.

But, what are we to make of this strange and tragic tale? The way in which it is told by Geoffrey of Monmouth implies that any literal interpretation will miss the point of the story. Only by examining the inherent symbolism in the account can we make any sense of it all. Certainly, the sexual overtones are apparent. Guendolena desires Merlin and is prepared to suffer hardship to be with him, but Merlin rejects her. Why? The answer may be in the role that his sister Ganieda plays in the drama. She has assumed a more significant role in her brother's life, essentially because it is *not* sexual. Merlin considers himself to be beyond the physical plane and that must preclude any intimacy, particularly with a sensual flower maiden. He is now free to enter the final stage of his magickal life and become the seer, embracing wisdom and solitude in equal measure.

If we accept the allegorical nature of the tale, then we must accept that 'the planes are separate' and always must remain so. What Merlin achieves on the Inner Planes cannot be confounded with his behaviour on the earthly plane. Those who condemn Aleister Crowley for his many vices make this error. One can easily say he was a good magician and a bad man, but with reference to magick it is a meaningless statement. Magick cannot be expected to support any moral stance; that is not its nature or purpose. Whether Crowley was a sexual pervert or a heroin addict makes not the slightest difference to his persona on the Inner Planes.

Too often does society make arbitrary judgments of those who flout its often equally arbitrary conventions. Merlin was incarnated at the moment when he would be most instrumental in shaping the Divine Will. It may be that his being a magician aids him in paying off any karmic debts that have accumulated in his previous lives. If he is a transmitter of Divine Light, the magician might be regarded as being exempt from any earthly transgressions. It is a fascinating philosophical conundrum.

✷ Deliverance ✷

. . . the winds will bring you news and knowledge if you ask them properly. The Trees of the Wood will give you power, and the waters of the sea will give you patience and omniscience, since the Sea is a womb that contains a memory of all things.

—ROBERT COCHRANE

Sacred Well

In a temporary respite from his fevered wanderings, Merlin is to be found at the top of a mountain in a grove of hazel trees. Hazel is associated with magick. The wands of this tree and eating of the nuts are said to confer wisdom. It is the beginning of the end of suffering for Merlin. Soon he will have his power restored. Magick will never desert the magician. He might feel that he has been abandoned by Thoth, the great god of magick, but this is never so. It is only in the *conscious mind* that despair racks him. Upon the Inner Planes, Merlin still retains, as always, his power and strength. The conscious mind may be affected by the tides of the unconscious, but what appears to be happening on that plane is merely the stuff of illusion. Music is the most transcendental of the arts and it is the sound of the lyre that soothes Merlin's troubled soul. A minstrel plays to him on the mountain top and calms his soul. The lyre is associated with Mercury, as we have learned, and he is also the god of magick. In its power to affect and alter the inner vision through the emotions, music is akin to magick.

Calmed by music, Merlin is then either told, or senses himself, the whereabouts of a sacred spring whose waters will cure him. He bathes his fevered head in these waters and his reason returns, his mind immediately becoming clear once more. It is almost as if that quality of reflection, which is the nature of water, forces Merlin to confront his true self. Water, the negative/yin element, has cooled the raging fire in Merlin's brain. Merlin immediately comes down from the mountain in a gesture that symbolizes his return to the world. But no longer is he the mentor of kings or a trusted adviser at court. He has become the true wild wizard of nature. Now he is a magnificent figure, and all are in awe of his magick.

Wells have always been associated with regeneration and rebirth. In old German, *well* and *origin* are the same word. Springs are lunar and sacred to the Goddess. In the Celtic tradition their protector is Epona, 'The Divine Horse' or 'The Great Mare'. When depicted in human form she has a horse at each side of her. The goddess Bride will be her successor. The spirit of Imbolc, she has her own well at Bride's Mound near Glastonbury. In another tradition, Ishtar is the ruler of springs; she is a fierce but sensual goddess, a feisty daughter of Venus. She raises the *kundalini* from the well, and the Great Serpent winds its coils about the entrance.

In a long poem, Taliesin, the Celtic bard, describes all the sacred springs of the world that he has known. The waters at some of them are beneficial while at others they may carry a curse. He mentions a spring in the region of Campania that is reputed to cure barrenness and to take away madness. Merlin's affliction was certainly that, a wasting of the mind. In the *Prophecies*, the sayings often attributed to him, Merlin speaks of a time when Britain undergoes purification through the ministries of the Goddess. As one who personifies the hidden magick of that country, he has been purified by the Goddess. We too must decide whether or not we have conquered our innermost fears and undergone purification. If we have truly succeeded in doing this then we have made *the self* subservient to the magickal will. *Conscience* is relevant here, a word derived from *consciousness* and *science*—to know the truth and the Divine Will simultaneously. To act *according to one's conscience* is to agree to let one's will be ruled by the highest powers.

Initiation

Merlin has been transformed by his experience. He accepts that the magickal consciousness is his only reality. With the realization that existence is wholly temporal, one concludes that the universe was not created simply for the convenience of humanity. The cosmos cannot be defined; neither can they be controlled. Their real nature will always defy reason and science. All the great thinkers resigned themselves to admitting that they knew nothing. Perhaps they are grateful that they cannot find the answers to what others consider to be important questions. Debate upon the meaning of life or the nature of God is, while diverting, no longer the path to wisdom. We should be aware that what we know of *ourselves* is only one version of how we really are. The *inner being* knows far more about the reasons that we are attracted or repelled by individuals. Employing the power of intuition always makes life easier; it links humanity with the Divine. We should cultivate our rapport with the Otherworld as often as we are able to do so. Surrendering to its might is essential for any magickal development. Our goal should be to develop a technique to slip effortlessly between these two worlds.

Now, Merlin has discovered once more the poetry of life, and this has bestowed upon him a new vision. He has felt anew the humanity inherent in the world and cast aside the persona of the beast. His mind is clear, his vision pure. Why should we not view his revelations with the detachment of a scientist? We can then define the fundamental difference between illumination and illusion. True visions reflect *beauty*, particularly *transcendent beauty*. The saint sees with 'the eyes of the soul'. Mere gazing at the material world gains us nothing; we might as well be lost in a fog. Merlin's progress towards the greater wisdom is of one who desires to *see*, not as a wild man but as a sober one.

When we approach death, it is not always the cessation of life that causes us the greatest anxiety, but the preparation for our going. Before his end, a Catholic will request the Last Rites to be administered by a priest. This final Holy Communion is known as the *Viaticum*, literally 'provision for the journey'. Similar preparations, though with an entirely different philosophy, are set out in great detail in the Tibetan Book of the Dead. This fascinating work sets out instructions for the soul as it experiences forty-nine days of changing phenomena until the time for its reincarnation. The Christian yearns to enter a state of grace, the Buddhist to gain 'Clear Light', and even the humblest soul longs for an everlasting peace at 'the going down of the sun'.

Undergoing death as a *sacrifice* is a spiritual theme common to many cultures. The notion of gaining knowledge as a result of sacrifice features prominently in Teutonic mythology. Odin (or Woden) gains the secret of the runes as a result of hanging upside down from *Yggdrasil*, the World Tree, the Norse conception of the force which sustains Heaven and Earth. This ritual death lasts nine days, nine being significant as it is the square of three. This *Trinity* appears to feature often in mythology, as it does in Christianity (Father, Son, and Holy Ghost), the triune deity of the Egyptians (Osiris, Isis, and Horus), and the Brahman, Vishnu, and Shiva of the Hindus.

The *Spear of Destiny* is not exclusive to the West, occurring as it does in Eastern culture and in the Christian tradition. As a seer, Merlin is renowned for his magickal staff, which sometimes gives him the appearance of The Hermit in the Tarot. The staff has an equal power to the wand, and both have been a badge of office since ancient times. Hermes owns the *Caduceus*, while the loop of the *Ankh* is held by the gods of ancient Egypt and is the symbol of life. It represents too the combined power of Isis and Osiris, the womb and lingam combined. Thoth, the god of magick, holds his staff with the same authority that Merlin will come to do in another era. There is much to link these two figures, as we have discovered. They both represent the will made manifest tempered by the presence of the universe.

Stargazer

In our own times the science of astrology has fallen into some disrepute. It is regarded as merely another column in a newspaper or with contempt by those who consider themselves to be 'rational'. It is hard to believe that, along with alchemy, astrology was once considered to be one of the *great mysteries*. John Dee, astrologer to Elizabeth I and her court, decided when her coronation should take place. Only when a favourable horoscope had been plotted did the queen agree to her crowning. The celebrated English scientist Sir Isaac Newton was also a devotee of astrology. When chided about his interest by his contemporaries, Newton replied, 'I have studied the subject, sir, you have not'. William Blake, encouraged by his contemporary John Varley, an eccentric astrologer, also held the science in high regard. Their mutual interest produced

A *Treatise on Zodiacal Physiognomy*, with a text by Varley and engravings by Blake.

For Merlin, astrology/astronomy was an important tool, as is evident when he requests his sister Ganieda to have an observatory built at a high point in the forest. This episode is taken to mean that Merlin has left his frenzied ways behind and has returned to reason in the way of investigating the Heavens. We must not assume that the kind of stellar research Merlin followed would be in any way identical to our own understanding. As always, Merlin adheres to his own idiosyncratic methods, and he may have incorporated the Arabic and Egyptian influences with which he was familiar. Yet he still embraces the fundamental tenet of astrology—events on Earth are reflected in the Heavens.

Merlin confides to Ganieda that he will spend the summer close to nature and in the winter take up residence in the observatory. In esoteric lore the Winter Solstice is considered to be the time to remove any part of the personality that is not essential to the Higher Self. Merlin observes the Heavens at the Winter Solstice, aware that the souls of the ancients are with him. It is possible that some stone circles are aligned specifically to study the constellations at that particular season. Merlin's observatory with its 'seventy doors and seventy windows' has similarities to a stone circle, particularly if the doors represent the spaces between individual stones. The number seventy may be aligned to the seven planets, which are in turn linked to the seven psychic centres, or chakras, of the body. Whatever the numerical basis of Merlin's astrology, it reflects the workings of his mind and his determination to understand and subsequently to control the natural forces of nature.

It is not surprising that the appearance of great stars in the Heavens brought great trepidation to those who observed them in the Dark Ages. One such, observed as Uther was riding out to do battle with the Saxons, seems a case in point. Even allowing for a certain amount of lyrical licence, the sight must have been quite startling, as this contemporary description demonstrates. The star was apparently:

> ... of marvellous bigness and brightness, stretching forth one ray whereon was a ball of fire spreading forth in the likeness of a dragon and from the mouth of the dragon issued forth two rays, whereof the one was of such great length as that it did seem to reach beyond the regions of Gaul and the other, verging toward the Irish sea, did end in seven lesser rays.[4]

Merlin, when called upon to interpret this phenomenon, confidently announced that it foretold the death of Aurelius and the coming of Arthur. The seven-rayed element of the heavenly light, he maintained, was certain to signify some future dynasty.

Saturn, which traditionally rules both Capricorn and Aquarius—respectively the dark and light sides of this

---

4. Geoffrey of Monmouth, *Histories of the Kings of Britain*, trans. by Sebastian Evans. (London: J. M. Dent & Sons, 1928), p. 143.

planet, casts its baleful presence over the winter months. It commences to do this at the Winter Solstice. Given Merlin's link with the planet Mercury, we may profitably investigate the link Merlin has with Mercurius, the alchemical personification of the *prima material*. Winter is the season of Earth, the North, and Midnight. All have the essence of stillness. The period also has within it the celebration of Christmas—the birth of the Messiah. Both Merlin and Mercurius have been compared to Christ and the Anti-Christ. Merlin's studies of the Heavens are taking him into a higher realm of transcendence, beyond duality and into a symbiosis of nature, one that is the realm of the greater Truth.

The symbolism within the constellations was familiar to the tribes of Europe. To them, the Stag was a representation of the Sun. This animal features prominently in Merlin's life, and Mercurius is known as the *cervus fugitives*—the fugitive stag. The constellation of Ursa Major lies in the North and indicates the position of Polaris, the North Star. The Bear, a representation of Arthur, is also to be found in this quarter of the Heavens. Of the planet Saturn, one final reference may be of value in its bearing upon the Quest for the Holy Grail: Merlin appears to Perceval carrying a sickle, a symbol of Saturn. The implication is that Perceval's psyche is flawed, and therefore he is not worthy of succeeding in the Grail Quest.

Our ancestors were fascinated by that formation of stars known as the Northern Cross. They knew it as 'the goose', while later generations would referred to as *Cygnus*—the swan. Perhaps this is a reference to its rider *Cailleach*, the crone, who rules the winter months. A symbol of the soul, the magnificent swan was revered by the Celts and the variations in its flight were the basis of their divinations. The swan is associated with both the Sun and Mercury. The notion that a swan flies in the air, swims in water, and nests upon the earth also makes it a metaphor for shapeshifting. In Celtic mythology the children of the sea god Lir were transformed into swans. The following correspondences may be of interest to our study. They represent my own view of zodiacal affinities based upon the individual characters in the Arthurian tales. Various Tarot correspondences are also included. It should be remembered that a neat table of attributions is almost impossible to compile, and in my view that is an affirmation of any esoteric system, not a weakness:

King Arthur: Aries/Leo/Capricorn (The Emperor/
  Strength/The Sun)
Guinevere: Taurus (The Empress)
Merlin: Gemini/Virgo (The Magician/The Hermit)
The Fisher King: Pisces (The Hanged Man/The Moon)
The Lady of the Lake: Cancer (The High Priestess/The
  Chariot/Justice)
Morgan le Fay: Scorpio (Death)
Elaine: Pisces/Virgo (The Hermit)
Lancelot: Scorpio/Capricorn (Death/The Devil)

Galahad: Sagittarius (Temperance)
Perceval: Aquarius/Pisces (The Star/The Hanged Man)

Seer

His time of trauma over, Merlin passes into the final phase of his life, that of sage and seer. His wisdom becomes legendary, his demeanour benign. Gone are the days when he might have dispatched the enemies of Arthur by casting a single spell. Certainly, he has caused the king to own Excalibur and thus provides the means for being victorious in battle. Merlin, as all magicians must, exists in a world that is not swayed by notions of good and evil. This does not mean he is amoral, far from it. The manner in which the magician regards a situation, and how he behaves, determines all. Our fate always hangs by the thinnest of threads. Few, if any of us, can accurately predict the future. Merlin is a seer—literally he has the gift of *seeing*. Not everyone upon the magickal path possesses the skill of Merlin. This wizard possesses more than mere psychism; he is the great prophet whose talent for prediction was once sought by kings.

Merlin is also aware that the world he has known for so long will soon disappear, in an apocalyptic end. Who knows how many worlds end just as dramatically as will the Kingdom of Logres? Merlin has the advantage of being the architect, Adam, and Archangel of his own Eden. It is also pertinent to speculate on the future incarnations that Merlin will enjoy. He first appears as Roger Bacon, the thirteenth-century monk who believed, among other notions, that the world was round when most of the population of the planet most emphatically did not. Bacon knew how to manufacture gunpowder but would not make his secret public for fear of the consequences. He predicted the invention of the hot air balloon, the flying machine, spectacles, the telescope, and the microscope.

Francis Bacon, who shared a surname with Roger Bacon, was one of the great thinkers of the sixteenth century and numbered among his friends Edmund Spenser, Christopher Marlowe, and Sir Walter Raleigh. Francis Bacon's writings inspired Hobbes, Bentham, and Locke. He also invented modern cryptology and used this art to good effect in constructing codes which he employed when writing. These concealed, and revealed when decoded, the great political secrets of the day. Bacon foretold the settling of America in his treatise *The New Atlantis*, and his role in founding the New World was instrumental. He believed that the character of the United States of America, as it was to become, should embody a true spirit of freedom and enlightenment. As the founder of modern Freemasonry, Bacon inspired the men whose signatures are upon the Declaration of Independence. Of the fifty-six men who signed, all but three were Freemasons.

In his next incarnation Merlin was reborn as Saint Germain. That extraordinary figure had also been a citizen of Atlantis—*The High Priest of the Violet Flame*. Incarnated in the sixteenth century, he was one of the great figures of England and Europe. Proficient in the art of music, writing, languages, and painting, he was the personal friend of Voltaire and Rousseau. He founded Rosicrucianism and travelled extensively, perhaps reaching Tibet on his travels.

The breadth of the character of Merlin defies description. The songs attributed to Taliesin, variously described as the pupil or companion of Merlin, or even his alter ego, have a marvellous, otherworldly quality. They epitomize very succinctly, and far better than any prosaic description, the spirit of Merlin as a man of vision and transcendental experience:

> I have been many shapes ...
> I have been a narrow blade of a sword;
> I have been a drop in the air;
> I have been a shining star;
> I have been a light in a lantern ...
> I have journeyed as an eagle;
> I have been a string of a harp;
> I have been enchanted for a year on the foam of water;
> There is nothing in which I have not been.

This amalgam of wonder, dream, and destiny is epitomized in our fairy stories, which often contain sorrow and failure, but always accompanying these elements is a fleeting glimpse of joy. We have come full circle, back to a world where the hat with stars on it and the bumbling, lovable figure beneath it shines eternally. But there is always a hint of Darth Vader's dark side!

✴ Lady of the Lake ✴

. . . Certain timeless ideas, which have been submerged
and subdued for a long time, are making their appearance
once again. In that respect we're living in very interesting
times as the Chinese would say. Interesting times, spiri-
tually powerful times, always cast a great shadow. There
will also be great difficulties . . .

—STEPHAN A. HOELLER

Dark Goddess

It is Morgan le Fay who will lead Arthur into the Otherworld as he is dying and Nimmue who will send Merlin into the void. Some say that these two enchantresses are one and the same, although it seems apparent that Morgan has the darker aspect. She provides an insight into how the feminine psyche is presented in the Arthurian tales. To Merlin, Water is the Goddess of the Lake, and the Wind purifying thought. Morgan is the Queen of Faery and also Death. The gender of Death is a moot point, though in his fantasy novels Terry Pratchett portrays Death, very convincingly, as male. But in the Arthurian tales, Morgan is as a Norse Valkyrie, one who takes the souls of dead warriors to Valhalla. It is she who will take Arthur to Avalon in her bark, the coracle of Cerridwen, for being of the Isis cult she ferries the dead to the underworld herself. Morgan le Fay may indeed be Persephone, the Queen of Hades and of the highest rank among the deities. She is certainly Hecate, the chthonian goddess of magick, and certainly capable of casting spells in pursuit of revenge.

Schooled in magick, Morgan certainly was. Her first master is a shadowy figure, so dark as to be to all intents invisible. We know almost nothing about him except that, like Merlin with Arthur, he was one who was anxious to oversee the birth of certain individuals. In this instance it was Morgan le Fay. In her youth she was summoned to the power centre of the Inner Temple within the sacred kingdom of Avalon. It was in that secret place that she learned her magick. She lived in a timeless state where she had no awareness of anything other than the great forces to which she slowly but surely became attuned. There is much of Nephthys, the dark sister of Isis, about Morgan. Perhaps there is more of the Queen of Heaven in Nimmue than in Morgan. Certainly Morgan is not above using her powers for her own ends, a proceeding generally not considered wise in the world of magick. Her will is almost invincible, and she displays many of the traits that we associate with the astrological sign of Scorpio.

In the modern system, Scorpio is ruled by Pluto, which in mythology was the ruler of Hades, the Underworld. Secrets, treasures, and the deepest of emotions are hidden there. Pluto also represents the catharsis in life, the purging of unwanted and therefore debilitating ideas and feelings. Revenge too is part of the Scorpio/Pluto world, and Morgan or Morgen is known as the *Apple Woman*, who distributes poisoned apples in an apparently wanton act of vengeance against humanity. The character of the Wicked Queen who features in many fairy tales is her legacy to children's literature and folk tales. Morgan also presides over the three springs of Life, Desire, and Death.

As her teacher, Merlin also taught Morgan le Fay much magick. During their time together the wizard came under the enchantment of Morgan and yearned for her. It is said that Merlin's nature was half-human and half-animal. The human half was female; the other was the Priapic god Pan, who is incapable of love and only feels lust. In Morgan le Fay it is the reverse: she is the wanton female who preys upon those men who are weak or foolish enough to be enticed by her. She is *La Belle Dame Sans Merci* of Keats' celebrated and evocative poem. It is her overwhelming charms that cause Arthur to couple with Morgan le Fay one fateful Beltane. The night, bewitchment, youth, and perhaps wine are the volatile elements in this affair. It has also never been made clear whether the protagonists of this passionate encounter knew, at the time, the identity of the other party.

Whatever the circumstances, and whether motivated by jealousy or revenge, in the years following, Morgan seems intent on thwarting the king's plans at every turn. She even goes so far as to attempt to steal Excalibur. After bewitching the guards at Camelot one night, Morgan succeeds in entering the king's bedchamber. Discovering that Arthur sleeps with the mighty sword firmly in his grasp and if he were to wake she would be instantly slain, she contents herself with stealing the scabbard. Of this, Merlin once asked of Arthur:

'Like ye better the sword or the scabbard?'

'I like better the sword', said Arthur.

'Ye are the more unwise, for the scabbard is worth ten of the sword; for while ye keep the scabbard upon you ye shall lose no blood, be ye ever so sore wounded . . . '[5]

On discovering the theft, Arthur sets off in pursuit, and Morgan le Fay, knowing he will overtake her, rides to a 'lake on the plain'. Once there she throws the scabbard far out into the water. Its heavily bejewelled patterning ensures that it will sink. She then turns herself and her followers into stone so they will be invisible. The loss of the scabbard immediately makes Arthur vulnerable to any hurt and signifies his ultimate downfall.

Another version of the tale has Morgan le Fay succeeding in appropriating both sword and scabbard, which she presents to Accolon, her lover. Arthur is then forced to fight a duel against him. Without Excalibur at his disposal, he is powerless against his foe. It is Nimmue who saves him by causing Accolon to drop Excalibur at the moment when he is about to deliver a death blow to the king.

Nimmue

Tales abound of the union of a mortal man and an immortal female—stories which invariably end in tragedy.

---

5. Sir Thomas Malory, *Le Morte Darthur: The Winchester Manuscript*. (Oxford: Oxford University Press, 1998), p. 30. Other editions are also available.

The most well-known involves Gwyn, a farmer's son, who pines for a water nymph he has once seen on the shore of the lake near his home. After a year has passed she returns, and when he declares his love she agrees to marry him, having first obtained her father's permission. A handsome dowry is offered, 'as many sheep, cows , goats, and horses as you can count in a single breath', but there is one proviso. Her husband must never strike her and if he does, warns the father, then 'she will return to me and bring in her wake all that she possesses'. The couple are wed and remain happily so for the time it takes to be blessed with three sons. Unfortunately, the husband does fall prey to temper and strikes his wife three times, so the father's stricture comes true, with indeed tragic results. On the third blow the wife immediately returns to the lake, which swallows her up. The distraught husband follows her into the water, only to be drowned.

The name Nimmue, as many characters in the Arthurian tales do, has multiple variations: Nimue, Niniane, Nyneve, Nimuehu, or even Vivienne and Vivianne. She is also Bride of the Celts, who is virginal and pure, a healing goddess who gives succour to all in travail. The father of Nimmue was Dyonas, the godson of Diana the Huntress. The 'Lake' was in Brittany and known as the 'Lake of Diana', so as a child Nimmue knew the woods and rivers of Diana's kingdom. The goddess one day predicts that Nimmue will win the love of the wisest man in the world. This 'water sprite' is in essence yet another Atlantean figure who is part of the great matriarchal culture that held sway in that place. Her kind, the 'faery women', have already taken up residence in Britain, even before Merlin arrives at the sacred isle with Ygraine. Their role then was to demonstrate to a relatively primitive culture that the ways of magick were ever present and had control of the forces of existence.

The world of fairy existed in harmony with the mortal universe for quite some time. The influence of Christianity eventually became so insidious that ordinary people were not permitted to acknowledge, let alone embrace, the old ways. It was considered 'wicked' to 'believe in fairies', and the imposing of guilt combined with ridicule in heavy doses is a guaranteed method of destroying a faith in anything.

The Celts are one of several cultural groups that have a lively fairy tradition. The Irish are particularly associated with the 'little people', who, diminutive though they may be, are always powerful. Traditionally they wear green so as to blend in to the landscape, though the red cloaks they also sport announces their presence to mortals. The beneficial power of fairies appears to be as an aid for growth of animals and plants. It as if the fairy presence somehow encourages vitality. Certain mediums can see the aura or spirit of trees, so it seems reasonable that the fairy kingdom is the physical expression of this aspect of nature. Fairies take an interest in the domestic life of humans, applauding the dutiful maid and helping her in invisible ways to be the epitome of neatness and cleanliness. In Qabalistic terms, Netzach is the Sephiroth of the Fairy Queen while Hod is Puck. The Queen of Elfland has fifty-nine silver bells on her bridle. The significance of the number seems lost to us now. Perhaps the numerologist might suggest that when the number is added laterally it totals fourteen, which is a double *heptad*—seven being a mystical number.

In our own times these fairy beings can still be contacted, and 'sensitive' individuals often do so. Their presence in ancient woods and places of power can be felt quite easily even by those who may not actively be seeking them. Tales are still told of the 'fairy band' whose music entices travellers to follow them into strange and lonely places where they succumb to an unnatural sleep. Fairies seem to be abroad mostly on a summer's eve when a glint amongst the trees betrays their presence. It is well to know that the intentions of the fairy race are not always for the benefit of humanity, and many people have heartily regretted their association with these creatures from another time. For it is their attachment to the past that makes them dangerous. They cannot ever change to become part of our own times, and so they wish to take mortals into their own realm. Those who are flattered by the attentions of fairies and accompany them seldom return from that enchanted kingdom.

The Arthurian Tales span the change of consciousness of man and his ultimate failure to secure the spiritual salvation of the Grail. The function of the Lady of the Lake in the Arthurian tales relates not only to Merlin but indirectly to Arthur, or rather what a king represents. By presenting the youthful monarch with Excalibur, she is directing his untamed virility into a transcendental force. That is her intention and had it succeeded, or rather had Arthur acted in a different manner, all would have been well. The acquisition of Excalibur should have awakened the female element in Arthur and given him the polarity that Merlin owns. This was not to be. His incestuous coupling with Morgan le Fay and his inability to relate to Guinevere his queen amply demonstrate that his spiritual growth remains stunted throughout his life. There is much to be said for the view that his youthful lust becomes a debilitating impotence, and it is he who is the Fisher King.

To return to our theme of the union of mortal and immortal, the 'Lady of the Lake' may once have been married to a mortal. Nothing is known of him except his honorary title *Emrys of Powys*. This is one of the titles owned by Merlin, so it may have been passed on to him. The actual *Lake* provides us with another dimension of meaning, for it is the astral plane and only those who truly acknowledge this otherworld can be privy to its secrets. In Qabalistic terms it is Yesod, the dominion of the Moon, presided over by Isis, who sits before the veil. Merlin is obviously associated with the Sephiroth of Hod. The planetary correspondences are Mercury and the Moon, respectively. The Qabalah path between the Sephira is represented by the Tarot card of the Sun, the ultimate cosmic energy.

The character who presents Arthur with Excalibur is a different 'Lady of the Lake' than the lover of Merlin. The former is the foster mother of Lancelot, abandoned when his father's kingdom was ravaged by a rebellion. This tale bears a great similarity to the Greek myth of Thetis, a sea nymph who raises Achilles, also a great warrior. The husband of Thetis is Peleus, and in some versions of the tale of Nimmue she takes the knight Pelleas as her lover. Thetis gives Achilles a magickal shield and armour to protect him, as Lancelot is later to be given protection by a magickal ring, the gift of Nimmue. Some resemblance to the tale of Melusine is also apparent. She is one of three daughters, raised in Avalon, who acquires a serpent's tail as punishment for imprisoning her own father. She marries, and her secret is discovered by her husband, who has spied upon her while she is bathing. Melusine immediately turns into a dragon and flies away.

Lancelot does not even know his own name and does not do so until he journeys to King Arthur's court at the behest of Nimmue. There, on meeting Guinevere, he immediately falls in love with her and gains his celebrated title. The ring that Nimmue gave Lancelot has the power of resisting enchantment, and he subsequently uses this magickal artefact when he rescues Guinevere in a later escapade with the queen. Nimmue also gives Guinevere the gift of a magickal shield which is split. The image painted upon the shield is of a knight and lady kissing, but their lips cannot touch because of the split. When their love is consummated, the shield will be made whole. This Nimmue does not suffer such a pleasant fate, being murdered by Sir Balin. That knight is then cursed, and his rash behaviour in the castle Carbonek is one of the causes of the kingdom becoming the Waste Land.

Innocence

It is said that when he became a very old man Merlin retired with Ganieda, his sister and protector, to the forest. Whether his straying from her protection brought about the denouement in the tale is uncertain. It seems that the wizard must face one more challenging episode in his life. The often accepted version of this time in Merlin's last days makes him out to be an old dotard deluded by the wiles of a nubile nymph. That view is far too glib, and we would be better employed looking for deeper meanings in the tale. Firstly, did Nimmue always foster the same intentions towards Merlin? Or was her path determined by Merlin's infatuation after he had come upon her bathing in a forest spring? It seems he may have been entranced by her beautiful form as she is equally taken with his magickal power. As the old saying has it 'Man desires woman, and woman desires man's desire'. The devotion of Merlin to Nimmue seems genuine. Nimmue is said to have promised not only her undying love but her favours as well to the wizard. Myths often echo previous myths, as when Isis obtained the secret name of Ra by nefarious means. With that knowledge she gained the ultimate power of magick.

Thomas Bulfinch in his *Mythology* depicts the following exchange between our protagonists:

'Sir, I would that we should make a fair place and suitable, so contrived by art and by cunning that it might never be undone, and that you and I should be there in joy and solace'.

'My lady, I will do all this'.

'I would not have you do it, but you shall teach me, and I will do it, and then it will be more to my mind'.

'I grant you this'.

Thus Merlin seals his fate and then, like the unicorn, goes on to put his head in Nimmue's lap. In mythology the unicorn places his horned head in the lap of a virgin, the tradition being that it is only an innocent who can gain the creature's trust. It is a virgin who tames him. The sexual overtones of this scenario are anything but subtle. Yet Nimmue will not give herself to Merlin, for she knew he was 'a devyl's son'. The story continues:

And a sleep
Fell upon Merlin like death, so deep . . .

Merlin wakes in the bedchamber, forever a prisoner in the enchanted tower. He never leaves it, though it is said that Nimmue visits him from time to time. It is as if Merlin has been sent to a retirement home for old wizards! Arthur sees his trusted companion only once more. Merlin tells him in a vision that the destiny of the Round Table is to search for the 'Sacred Graal'. Merlin adds that the knight who will succeed in the quest has already been born. He is Galahad, the son of Lancelot, conceived through sorcery. The setting for this final chapter is the Forest of Broceliande, near the city of Rennes in Brittany. Many of the episodes in the Arthurian tales are said to be set here. Scenes involving Morgan le Fay in the *Val sans Retour* and Gawain's encounter with the Green Knight have a Breton backdrop. *Tumuli* and stone *alignements* abound there, and an air of mist and mystery is strong in that country. The Bretons have a strong affinity with the Celts of Britain, and many visitors to this part of France remark upon the similarity of the landscape to Cornwall, a county in England known for its Arthurian associations.

Merlin's love for Nimmue, which effectively ends his association with Arthur, is far more than folly. It is the necessary transformation of the old star magick into the era of the wise woman. In the *Vita Merlini*, Nimmue is described as being a child of twelve years old, yet she is most obviously a young maiden. We might conclude that the number twelve may be regarded as a symbol of the zodiacal months in a year, and the maiden to be a version of Prosperine.

More than a touch of allegory is present in the way that ancient and modern magick meet. We might begin to see the entombment of Merlin as a sacrificial act. In ancient lore the priest/king voluntarily merges with the earth. He does this willingly in the knowledge that the starry Heavens are within and not without. An alternative version of the tale has the two living happily ever after in their world of enchantment. This is blatantly a cop-out and misses the point entirely, for the new magick must replace the old shamanic ways. Merlin places himself willingly in the dark place of the spirit where he may be a guide for others who find themselves lost in its depths. In later times Merlin will become Puck—the Magician turned witty Fool, and his female counterpart Morgan le Fay will be Titania, the Queen of the Faeries.

Merlin, being a seer, knows what his fate is to be and it is important to realize that he simply accepts it. Such an *acceptance of change* is the essence of the concept of *Wyrd* (Old English, Saxon *wurd*; Old High German *Wurt*; Old Norse *urur*.) The term is now regarded as meaning *weird*, in the sense of odd or unusual, but that was not its original meaning. It is apposite that the *weird sisters* in *Macbeth* may have been based on the *Three Norse Goddesses of Destiny*. Let us examine this concept by first comparing Wyrd to the 'inexorable fate' of the ancient Greeks. It can be seen that Wyrd does not follow that approach because it proposes that our past, both personal and ancestral, affects us continuously. What we have done, and what others have done to affect us, is the sum of ourselves. Every choice we make in the present builds upon choices we have made before; this results in *Wyrd* being not the end, but the constant. 'Active fate' might be one way of looking at it.

Ancient peoples did not have a notion of linear time and supported the idea of a phenomenal universe rather than a causal one. If a man is doomed, nothing can save him. A stoic element permeates much Anglo-Saxon poetry, and the *zeitgeist* considered that if a man cannot avert his fate he should at least be stoical about it. Yet courage might tip the scales in the favour of an undoomed mortal, for 'fortune favours the bold' as the old saying goes. Whether we take heed of them or not, signs pointing to the true way are always there when it is necessary for us to make a significant choice.

Gateway

We find ourselves in an age when it is rare for the individual to reflect upon his or her death. Longevity is the norm and youth extolled as a virtue. In the Dark Ages people were constantly stalked by Death in the shape of famine, disease, and war. The flame of Life was expected to stay alight but briefly, and thus it did. Because we *know* we will die, a certain *unease* about our human condition is bound to make its presence felt. Yet if we accept that death shapes our life, then perhaps we may see the beauty of the latter that much clearer. If 'being there' is temporary and uncertain, then let us 'be' as fully as possible. How we fill our days is our choice. We may behave as a saint or debauch ourselves, the choice is ours. We fear death as we fear the future, for we see life as a linear construct—not a continuum, as we should. To have some understanding of what might lie beyond death was the motive behind any ancient ritual of initiation. The initiate would undergo an experience akin to death.

In the West we appear to favour having one foot out of the grave. The idea that our heroes come back to rescue us when we are in danger appeals to the Western mind. Our myths confirm this. The tale of King Arthur is the most powerful Western myth, one that has endured for over a thousand years, and its theme is return. The king sleeps, his knights with him, ready for the time when he is needed once more to vanquish his enemies and restore the kingdom. We like to believe that good triumphs over evil, love is supreme, and the world is a place of beauty and joy. Merlin has no fear of death. He has travelled too far and too many times into the Otherworld to be anxious about losing his hold upon the earthly plane. Magicians regard planes of existence as simply different from each other rather than one being better than another. Merlin is of the nature of Mercury and he is constantly moving in time and space, for restriction is anathema to the winged god.

The three stages of Merlin's life correspond to the Celtic threefold goddess, she who is personified as the Maid, the Bride, and the Crone. Merlin's birth and youth represent the maid; his marriage to Guendolena, the Bride; and his time as a seer, the Crone. On another level, the Maiden is a virgin whose gift is inspiration. She is associated with Briggida (Brigit), Athena, and Minerva. The Lover or Bride is fertility, linked to Guinevere. The Destroyer (Crone) represents death and prophecy and is the Morrigan or Morgan le Fay. This threefold theme continues to appear with reference to the deities.

In accounts of the old gods, grouped in a mighty triumvirate, are the God of Heaven, the God of the Primeval Deep, and the Lord of the Golden Age. They are all associated with the Moon through its phases. Observing these changes would have greatly impressed the Ancients. The Moon-Priest must undergo three initiations and make three sacrifices before he is accepted by Isis or Ishtar. Isis herself is known as 'Goddess of Heaven, Goddess of Earth, and Goddess of the Underworld'. This is her full title and one that is rarely heard outside of the Temple.

In a similar fashion to that of Arthur retiring with his knights to the caverns beneath Glastonbury Tor, Merlin vanishes into his cave on Bardsey Island off the coast of North Wales. He prudently takes with him the Thirteen Treasures of Britain. These are:

The Sword of Rhydderch, which burst into flame from hilt to tip.

The Hamper of Gwyddno, which was a cornucopia that could satisfy all.

The Horn of Bran, which provided any drink that was desired.

The Chariot of Arianrod, which gave transport to any destination.

The Halter of Clydno, which would conjure any steed.

The Knife of Llawfroded, which served many men at a table.

The Cauldron of Dyrnwch, which only boiled meat for the brave.

The Whetstone of Tudwal, which sharpened only a brave man's sword.

The Coat of Padarn, which fitted only the well-born.

The Dish of Thygennyd, which provided any food desired.

The Chessboard of Gwenddolau, which would play by itself.

The Mantle of Arthur, which gave invisibility to the wearer.

The Stone and Ring of Eluned, which granted conceal-ment from all.

✷ The Quest ✷

For 'tis the secret of the Grail
And evil can befall the man
Who talks of it in any way
Except the way it should be told.

—WAUCHIER DE DENAIN

Merlin's Gift

Merlin's gift to those whom he left behind was no comfortable memento. He presented the Company of the Round table with the ultimate symbol of a spiritual journey so great, that it was meant only for those who were worthy of the calling. It has since become the most potent search for salvation in history—the Quest for the Holy Grail. Merlin knew that if they succeeded this would be the ultimate achievement of the knights who served King Arthur.

Merlin will manifest the all-embracing principle of faith in the form of the Quest for the Holy Grail. Merlin has an understanding of all things feminine, and he is most certainly aware that the Quest is the search for the female element in creation. Being unaware of the Christian artefact that it will become, Merlin regards the 'Grail' as being the Cauldron of Cerridwen. Some say the wizard was even the son of Cerridwen in the guise of his alter ego Taliesin. Whether or not this is so, the old magick is still at the root of the Grail and thus will have a strong influence on the Quest.

The original 'Quest' was the physical experience of initiation. In the search for the 'vessel of power', Arthur leads his band to the Underworld for the purpose of being initiated into the mysteries. He follows the example of Osiris and Orpheus, who believed that only in the recesses of the subterranean world could the great secrets be learned. It is the abode of death, a place that to the Pagan mind holds no fear. By possessing the sacred vessel, the king demonstrates that he has power over life and death and qualifies to be a conduit for the ancestors to refuel the regal energies.

Because the vessel represents fertility, in the sense of well-being, the emotional, physical, and mental health of the tribe is dependent upon the leader/hero possessing the vessel. He assumes great power and status because he is the holder of the cup; he is the cup itself. If the power of the incumbent wanes, then the people lose their guardian, as the story of the Fisher King and the Waste Land will so dramatically demonstrate.

The history of the Grail is intimately linked to a belief in the existence of some sacred object owning mystical powers. This occurs in many cultures. The Chinese speak of a dragon that holds a pearl in its jaws, and the Syrians revered meteoric stones. The Philosopher's Stone, Jason's Golden Fleece—this is the prize awarded to the searcher for his diligence and courage. Eventually in these tales, the actual goal becomes more and more nebulous, the element of initiation within the Quest becoming much stronger. In the Arthurian tales, a location such as the Forest of Broceliande becomes a representation of the unconscious mind where the most fearful monsters reside. It is like the scene depicted on the Moon card of the Tarot, where the initiate must pass between the pylon gates, his gaze fixed firmly on the road ahead no matter what he may sense is lying in wait for him in the shadows. Eventually he gains the hills beyond. Even there he may encounter further challenges, but at least he has passed the first test. It seems that we have to know Hell in order to experience Heaven.

Traumatic experiences, sufficiently intense to alter our essential self, appear to be a necessary condition of spiritual progress. Only when we have undergone the longest and darkest of nights are we permitted to see the glory of the dawn. By undergoing such extreme sensations we are tested, and what is being measured is the strength of our spirit. Any explanation of the 'Grail', whatever it might represent, must have within it the notion of a greater awareness, which is a greater knowledge of the self.

By developing the ability to work with the unconscious forces, balance returns to life and illusion is avoided. Having a 'true perception' is particularly important in the twenty-first century, a time when falsity and artifice have almost become a way of life. It must be remembered that nothing is quite the same once the seeker has entered the Inner Worlds. It is not that she wishes to dwell there constantly (she knows she would be in error if she did), it is simply that the very knowing of this other existence gives a strength and purpose to her life. She now feels that she really is part of the universe and thus in total command of her existence. The shadows that once threatened her fall back. Her fear of the unknown disappears. Illusions still possess their glitter, but no longer is there the slightest chance that they will turn to gold.

The adept knows that constantly shifting levels of reality make up our consciousness, and we have the ability to colour and create them in any way we please. The creative imagination plays its part in all of this, composing a view that illustrates the place from where we originated—detailing the face of God. That countenance is a reflection of ourselves. We come to this plane through the grace of God, and the nature of God is *love*.

Holy Vessel

Chivalry was an attempt to leaven the brew of aggression that existed among young knights in feudal England. Jousting, often seen as a well-ordered display of prowess for the entertainment of the ladies of the court, was in reality often vicious brawling between rival gangs. It was the Church that encouraged the more civilised knights of the time to introduce rules of conduct that would contain the fighting spirit of aristocratic youth. It is against this backdrop that we must regard the birth of the Quest. A measure of its power is that the Grail may soften unruly hearts, even, it must be said, of those chosen to occupy a seat at the Round Table. Do these knights who undertake the Quest know that the purpose of the Quest is to discover the Grail (or the

Holy Spirit) within one's heart? If not, they will soon discover its essence or abandon their mission.

It is not surprising that the Grail was originally a vessel of the Underworld, for its nature is concealed. It is the womb, the Goddess herself. The Transition from Pagan prize to Christian icon is through the Virgin Mary, via her title *Stella Maris*—star of the sea. It is the Moon that rules the tides, and she is the essence of magick and the domain of the Goddess. It may be also that the grail, or cup (Water), is one of four great treasures. The other three are the Spear of Destiny (Fire), The Sword of Truth (Air), and the Oracular Stone (Earth). They are traditionally the gift of a Celtic queen, strongly suggesting that The Grail per se is exclusively part of the Western tradition. It may be relevant that the element of Water owns the West as its magickal direction.

The modern yearning for tangible proof of the *purpose* of the Grail has still to be satisfied, which rather implies that such a one-dimensional approach achieves nothing. The debate as to the precise nature of that artefact and its whereabouts has, over the years, spawned a vast literary oeuvre, and popular interest in the subject shows no sign of abating. Whether the Holy Grail is the actual Cup used at the Last Supper or the two cruets that contained the blood and sweat of Jesus Christ seems to be of less important than the *meaning* of this Holy of Holies. The Christian version of the Quest insists that the hero, in order to gain the Grail, must be the embodiment of purity. This was certainly not a prerequisite in earlier versions of the saga, when both hero and magician are more worldly figures, pragmatic in their methods. Merlin and Arthur are each an archetype in transition, and the later version of themselves will be very different, almost a dwindling in stature.

With the coming of Christianity, and the ousting of the Gnostic version of the faith, the goddess element became more and more marginalized. The Church, a patriarchal institution, naturally disapproved of any female element owning the same status as the Messiah. A subtle engineering of how this should be regarded meant inventing a version of female virtue that was based upon, yet radically altered, the idea of virginity. Originally, this element of the goddess was not maidenhood but innocence, which is neither male nor female. It is a quality essential to any spiritual being, and as Confucius says:

He who departs from innocence, what does he come to? Heaven's will and blessing do not go with his deeds.

Thus does the character of the Grail become associated with the Holy Virgin, the epitome of unsullied purity. Later, the Church, intent on removing *any* feminine element in the Trinity, began to show its disapproval even of this association. Both the Cathars and the Knights Templar, two sects whose beliefs were entwined with the Grail, were persecuted unmercifully. Their creeds were seemingly obliterated by the Catholic Church in Europe, though vestiges of their beliefs survived in the Rosicrucian society. As a result, from the Middle Ages onwards, the Grail disappears as a mainstream Christian icon. The most significant symbol of Christianity, although never entirely losing its power, suddenly becomes a *bête noire*.

As a myth, its power increased, and it appears, admittedly in a much modified form, as part of the service of the Eucharist. The Church adapted the notion of transmutation, or—in the case of the Catholic Church—transubstantiation, into its liturgy. This proceeding is much more akin to a magickal ceremony than the Communion Service of the Church of England. It must be said that through its priests the Catholic faith has, perhaps even unwittingly, preserved much of the magickal tradition over the centuries. It is as if the original 'cauldron', part of Merlin's Pagan ancestry, will not relinquish its power. In the guise of the Grail it recedes into a world of mist and romance. It is now a far cry from the Goddess' proffered cup, flowing with her fertility—oozing and earthy.

The Waste Land

In ancient tradition, the physical state of the kingdom was reflected in the welfare of the king. To this end he might even be ritually married to the tutelary earth goddess of the tribe. When the land is suffering, 'the crops fail and the trees lose their leaves', and it is believed by his people that the monarch has brought this about. The ailing kingdom has become an infertile and barren place. In

the Arthurian tales, this 'Waste Land' describes the par-
lous condition of Logres before its ultimate fall. What has
brought this about? The reasons are several, but mainly it
is Arthur's virtual rejection of Guinevere, the queen repre-
senting the earthly, and thus the fertile, aspect of the kingdom. Aligned with this is Arthur's failure to prevent the
growing passion between Guinevere and Lancelot. The
ravishing of the Grail Maidens by unknown knights is a
crime that cannot easily be forgiven. Lastly is the 'dolorous
stoke', the wounding of Pelles, or Pellean the Fisher King,
by Balin le Sauvage. A catalyst that signals untold disaster
occurs in other traditions as well. Shiva is attacked in the
woods by sages who think he is a madman, and Adonis is
gored by a boar. In both cases the land suffers.

In this instance the Fisher King, who is keeper of The
Hallows, is wounded with the Spear of Destiny, stolen by
Sir Balin from the sacred chamber in Pelles' castle. This
blasphemy occurs when he is searching for a weapon to
defend himself against Pelles' supposed attack. Balin enters the chamber where Joseph of Arimathea lies upon a
bed of gold. As this place is a symbolic representation of
the Sangreal, Balin has now profaned it with his presence.
As a result, the Hallows disappear, the land will become
barren, and the Grail will be lost forever. The age of Pisces
being personified by Christ, the Grail is also a Piscean
symbol. Both Arthur and the Fisher King will be denied
the Grail, and the disasters that will befall Arthur echo
the Fisher King's fate. Both kings will be condemned to a

place where there is, as Richard Barber phrases it, ' . . . no hint of magic, merely the stark reality of a land left prey to marauders . . . enemies are presumably at large, and because he cannot lead his army to fight them, his land is open to attack'.[6]

The presence of a negative force, constantly waiting for any opportunity to bring destruction, is what makes the Waste Land seem so sinister. As the kingdom in its pomp is the reflection of Heaven, so the Waste Land is the shadow of Hell. Balin's role in all this is that of the pathological victim.

In the Celtic tradition, the barren land is cursed, and that curse can only be lifted by a hero. Of the four knights (Lancelot, Bors, Perceval, and Galahad) who attempt to secure the Grail and fulfill the Quest, only Galahad succeeds and is the *Grail Hero*. Perceval fails by not taking the opportunity to ask the *Grail Question*. Lancelot is deemed not worthy because of his adulterous affair with Guinevere and Bors, although proving he is a virtuous knight, seems fated to be an onlooker. The Question that Perceval should have asked has been variously interpreted, but it is generally considered to be, 'Whom does the Grail serve?' A suitable answer has even been suggested, which is, 'The Old King whose heir you are'. The implication being that if Perceval had taken up his inheritance, fertility would have returned to the land. As we know, this does

---

6. Richard Barber, *The Holy Grail: Imagination and Belief.* (London: Penguin, 2004), p. 20.

not happen and it is Galahad who acquires the Grail. He and Bors depart with their prize to Sarras, a mystical island situated near Egypt. The name is possibly derived from the Greek word for Arab: *Saracen*. The Grail is then taken up to Heaven, and Galahad dies in ecstasy at the sight. Whether the return of the Grail to its divine resting place breaks the spell of the Waste Land is a moot point, as all the writings are ambiguous concerning this matter.

A variation in the earlier part of the tale has Perceval and Galahad exchanging roles. In the more accepted version Galahad immediately occupies the *Siege Perilous*, the place at the Round Table reserved only for a worthy knight, as soon as he enters Arthur's court. His expected death from divine retribution for such effrontery does not occur, and the other knights are suitably amazed. Galahad thus fulfills Merlin's prophecy as being the only knight who will secure the Grail. In another version it is Perceval who occupies the sacred seat, causing it to crack with a violent sound, and the era of the Waste Land begins at that moment. In this way the notion that Perceval is the classic Fool is more than hinted at, particularly when he merely gazes at the Grail when it is brought before him in the Grail Castle.

The actual location of the Grail Castle is said to be on the Isle at Avalon at Glastonbury, at the foot of Wearyall Hill. The lake that is the abode of the Lady is at Pomplarles Bridge, which is also known as *Pons Perilis*, the Bridge Perilous. The questing knight must cross this 'bridge of swords' before entering the Grail Castle. He will have spent the preceding hours in prayer at the chapel on Bride's Mound. In this night of vigil his armour is the Lower Self and his spurs the Higher Self. At dawn he approaches the bridge, a psychic gateway where all previous notions of reality must be set aside. The last journey of the soul involves the crossing of the river Styx and represents the passage from life to death, or from the realm of mortals to that of the gods. The most dramatic transition between worlds is contained in Norse mythology—the Rainbow Bridge (*Bifrost*, meaning "tremulous way"). It depicts the rainbow as the name suggests, but it may also have been a reference to the Milky Way. Whatever it represents, it is ultimately doomed to destruction when the fire giants thunder across it at *Ragnarok*, the end of the world.

Fall of the Kingdom

The changing seasons of the might be likened to the rise and tragic fall of Logres (*Lloegr*, Welsh for 'kingdom'). After their joyous summer engaged with the Quest, the melancholy autumn is the rift between the knights, and the raging winter is the end of the kingdom. We await the return of spring as we await the return of Arthur, but in this bleak season, treachery and black passions rise and engulf all reason. Knight battles against knight, friends become foes, and Arthur is about to die at the hand of Mordred, his own son. As the Chinese proverb tells us, 'The gem cannot be polished without friction, nor man perfected without trials'. In the Eastern tradition the purification of the innermost being involves the paying of debts acquired in past lives—balancing the karmic books. When we emerge into the place of 'knowing without thought', we have, with the ceasing of life, no earthly restraints upon the soul; it takes wing and returns to whence it came—Eternity. Love, which is the true energy within the Grail, is also eternal, within all things and present in every moment of existence, though we may not always perceive it.

Love and death are two themes that are often interwoven in these tales. Both are at the root of all mystery. We have one last riddle to solve—that of the actual death of Merlin. We know that he has been incarcerated in the Castle of Enchantment that Nimmue has built, but does he simply waste away, a doddering old man in the darkness of his own mind? We would suppose not. He is a wizard, and he will depart as a wizard. The death of Merlin, like his life, is a mystery. Whither does he return, if to anywhere? Does he become a spirit in the forest, returning to the godhead? Merlin is, in one sense, the essence of the Grail, so does he join with it in another realm? Many questions, and as with Merlin, only the limits of the imagination determine the answers. To gain some insight into his passing, we might examine the Celtic *Threefold Death*. This, like the Tibetan Book of the Dead, is a guide to achieving complete transcendence at death. In this way, no attachment to any of the four realms of the elements will remain.

To understand the ideas presented here, much will be gained from examining that most enigmatic of the cards of the Tarot, the Hanged Man. The state in which the apparently contented figure finds himself, or chooses to be in, is between two worlds. He is secured to his earthly support yet free to float in the aether. On his joining with the element of Air, he gains wings and flies. He is carried high, inspiration keeping him above the mountains, until, like Icarus, he eventually falls. Now he must encounter the change that will accompany his entry into the world of Fire. With his newfound illumination he is purified and transformed. His great energy, as if riding a mighty steed into the Sun, is like a magickal death and leads him to the next element in the chain.

The opposite force of Water now almost drowns him in her great blessing and purification. The River of Time washes away any past imbalance, and with this spiritual grace comes understanding. The healing cycle begins and continues into the realm of the final element, Earth, which draws sustenance from the deeps below. It is this realization of the material plane that brings the ultimate wisdom. Our sojourn within the consciousness of Malkuth leads ultimately to our ascending the Tree and returning to Kether, the Crown from where we began. Soon we will journey along the lightning flash once more through all ten Sephira while Malkuth beckons.

And so, Merlin in death has gained the ultimate state, his soul has brought him to the Limitless Light. He is at the fullest consciousness without consciousness—a paradox, one that attempts to define Nirvana. Let us simply say that Merlin in death is at his most alive. In life he was never far from a state close to death, and this awareness gave him his magickal power. He was a warrior and magician simultaneously, possessing equally the courage needed to fight for existence and the ability to surrender.

∗ Magickal Legacy ∗

Many people think that the East is the only home of occult-ism, but this is far from being the case. Every race has had, and still has, its traditional, guarded wisdom, revealed to the few and concealed from the many. Our own Western tradition traces its origins to Egypt, with tributaries from Chaldea, Greece, and the fierce Norse tradition.

—DION FORTUNE

Modern Magus

Forty years ago, Bristol Central Library in the South West of England was a very scholarly institution. It felt particularly so for a young man embarking on the path of magick. In the reserve stock of the library was a cornucopia of mystical material. The staff were not cavalier with these treasures; I was permitted only to examine John Dee's *Monas Hieroglyphica* while seated at a table strategically placed so as to be within the librarian's gaze.

And what did I glean as I ploughed my way through these grimoires and magickal diaries? For a certain ritual it was incumbent 'to buy an egg without haggling' before burying it at midnight in a churchyard; for another, fasting and the imbibing only of 'fresh dew' was necessary. I was fascinated by the minutiae of it all—and no mention of selling your soul to the devil, as I had feared, but many entreaties to live a pure life. All the magickal rituals employed the Holy Names. I was impressed. It was all a revelation.

Fortunately, most of the 'spells' in ancient grimoires do not work. By the law of averages some of them will, but even then no responsible magician would recommend their use. Karma comes into this, and 'payback time' definitely exists. Try to bend the universe to your will and you will end up being bent over backwards and tied up in knots. The magician can only alter consciousness in a manner that is concordant with the laws of the universe—so he does not break those laws. He knows he cannot successfully challenge them. Let us follow the development of magick from the Dark Ages until the present day; it is the only way that will give us a true perspective of the magickal practitioner and his art.

After the comfortable chaos of Paganism, the medieval mind reacted by desiring to impose order on the material and the spiritual. Both church and state became hierarchical and patriarchal. Perhaps in an inevitable reaction to this ethos, occult practice lapsed into charlatanism and disarray. With few exceptions, the sorcerer of the Middle Ages lived a squalid existence. He was generally despised and so fearful and isolated. Often libidinous, his only ambition was to attract women, acquire great treasure, and destroy his enemies. Evoking spirits and commanding them to do his will was the usual method of attaining such ends.

According to Crowley, to do this successfully the magician has to acquire all the virtues, but none of the vices, of each of the elements. Of *sylphs*, the creatures living within the element of Air, the magician must be prompt and active but not capricious; with fiery *salamanders* it is advised to be energetic and strong but not ferocious. Labour and patience are required to master the earthy *gnomes*, while grossness is to be avoided; and the watery *undines* demand fluidity without wantonness.

Evoking 'elementals' is a dangerous and unethical practice, and making contact with entities on the lowest levels of the astral planes, the haunt of wraiths and negative energies, is not recommended. Opening that particular gateway is always fraught with perils, but it is evident that no number of warnings can restrain the curious and the foolish from venturing where 'angels fear to tread'. *Evocation* for the reasons stated can never be free of pitfalls. The practice of *Invocation* might require study and the training of the magickal imagination, yet is by far the more wholesome practice and free of untoward happenings.

The spirits of Fire, Water, Earth, or Air can be detected by those sensitive enough to do so. One example is the watery elemental that hovers over a lake—a tangible mist, quite unlike the meteorological phenomenon. It is as well to remember that all things are alive. Rocks are life forms in trance, trees are sleeping. Animals are awake and humans conscious—that is the only difference between them. Pan, being half human and half beast, has his own unique quality. He is poised between deity and earth spirit. Although one cannot ignore his Priapic tendencies, a quality beloved of neo-Pagans, he is best regarded as the guardian of the natural world. His air of vitality and his nurturing of all life in the forest and beyond can be felt, particularly in places seldom visited by people.

These secret worlds are precious and powerful. If you are fortunate enough to have discovered any, then share their whereabouts with no one! To walk among trees and undergrowth that has not been 'managed' or even visited is a great privilege. The feelings encountered there are what the magician seeks to bind eternally to his heart. It is marvellous to encounter the same spirits that Merlin knew—for the ways of nature are timeless and inspiring.

Arthurian Magick

The Arthurian saga is eminently suited to magickal workings, because the interplay of its symbolism is wholly original and therefore possesses its own potency. The figures, situations, and truths are not allegorical, meaning that they have no comparison with existing individuals. The student of magick should engage totally with the figure, or figures, with which they feel a strong affinity. Let the Arthurian tales enter into your life and become part of your soul! Artefacts such as the Grail or any of the Hallows may also be used to good effect. I would recommend caution in any dealings with Morgan le Fay, as her ways of enchantment may be overwhelming for the novice. Lancelot betrays a heaviness that may not be welcoming, and identifying with Mordred should be avoided altogether.

The reader might wonder if I give unanimous approval to any thoroughly modern Merlin. My answer is that I didn't choose to follow magick; it chose me. I have always had companions from the other world since I was of an age to perceive them, though it was not until I became familiar with the world of magick that I realized who they may have been. I am part of the 1960s, a time when the mystical world was brought back into focus. It was not long before I wanted to find out if there was anybody else out there who saw things in the way I did. As a student I encountered T. S. Eliot's *The Waste Land*, and learned of Madame Sosostris and her 'wicked pack of cards'. That sent me scurrying off to buy a Tarot pack and a book on astrology, too, but I was still a babe regarding the ways of the occult. Somehow I was determined, for my own peace of mind, to dispel any juvenile impressions of black cats, evoking Beelzebub and the like. That happened when I met real magicians—stern, forbidding gentlemen and with many a tale to tell. I went on to avidly study the works of Dion Fortune, Aleister Crowley, and W. G. Gray, but it was Merlin himself who more than once stopped me straying into unprofitable areas of magick and put me back on the right path.

I have only to say that magick is a hard and always daunting way. Those who remain upon this path suddenly discover that their whole lives have changed and often very dramatically. Life can become very stormy indeed when the magickal forces wish to make a point! Old ways and even old friends are left behind, but hopefully the initiate realises that his or her development needed that shedding of unnecessary baggage. The other fundamental change for the apprentice magician is that all experiences start to have a significance in a way that they never did before. It is as if the universe has slowed down so its ways can be examined more closely. Even an ordinary thing like walking down the street has a different air about it, which can be summed up in one word—*awareness*.

By its nature, magick forces us to be aware. Aware of what is there, what is *really there*, and what *could be there* if we wanted it to be. Magick also determines an individual path for every mortal. No one is permitted to follow the same path as another. The light of the Masters may shine upon each and every one of us who practice it but not in quite the same way. To follow another magician for too long is like wandering in the forest on winding paths that in the end lead nowhere. We must not have too much concern with the *persona* or any other illusion of the many that are nurtured by the ego. Concealing one's real self with yet more layers of illusion is like wearing too many clothes on a hot day—unbearable.

The magickal adage 'Know thyself' is the keynote of magickal maturity. This universal insight bestows a sense of 'belonging', nurtures your outlook, and thus keeps you firmly on the path. A built-in warning system reminds you how to conduct yourself to prevent any straying into 'no man's land'. This signal can range from reminding you to pocket your front door key to telling you how to act in some awkward situation.

Magick is always useful and practical. It is the most valuable asset you can own. It also encourages you to employ different ways of looking at the world. This does not mean being indecisive; it means being open to change. Seeking alternatives and 'thinking out of the box' are good exercises for keeping the mind adaptable. Carlos Castaneda makes the point that nothing in our world is ever permanent and that we limit ourselves if all the time we try to define everything we see or hear. That is not to advocate a dreamy or romantic attitude. If such a state was detected in a pupil during their magickal training they were termed 'fairy-addled'—a splendid description.

There is a right time for the practising of magick and another, just as important, for a walk by the sea. Both may be equally valuable to the individual. It is very essential for the magician to live an 'ordinary life'. Particularly, he must not shun his responsibilities to those he cares for, namely his parents, his spouse or partner, and his children, friends, and neighbours. This element of earthly power is known as 'hearth magic', and the importance of its contribution to the well-being of the magician cannot be overestimated. The other consideration is that energy can be easily dissipated, particularly magickal energy. The practitioner should be disciplined, ordering his existence and exerting as much control as he is able over the business of life. The magician learns when he should 'turn off' his power. Because the conscious world is a reflection of the unconscious, subtle vibrations are always to be preferred to twanging constantly upon the magickal instruments.

In *knowing himself* the magician is also aware of how others perceive him. No true magician is ostentatious about his calling. If he does succumb to such exhibitionism, then he is a mere poseur, and deserves only contempt. The magician makes certain, too, that he lives in the present. He dismisses past events as being times long gone and does not waste his energies with fantasies about the future. Living in the moment is his aim, for he knows that the present is *the moment*. The magician learns to seize the 'right now' because he has learned that this, his own 'present moment', exists beyond the dictates of time. In knowing this he has total mastery over what *occurs* at any given moment. Much of the real power of magick is contained in this idea, and the student would be well-advised to reflect upon it.

Gandalf

The author and academic J. R. R. Tolkien represents a certain English archetype, and like his creation Gandalf, he is made of the stuff of myth himself. A pipe-smoking professor at Oxford who rode his bicycle to the pub to meet his friend C. S. Lewis . . . it is all too good to be true! Yet this retiring, stoic Catholic, a veteran of the First World War, wrote the greatest and most timeless mythical tale of the twentieth century. The work was made into a trilogy of films and directed with great élan by Peter Jackson. Tolkien's vision found an entirely new following, most of whom, it must be said, had never read the book. It was a great popular success, containing fictional characters as memorable as Sherlock Holmes or Mr. Pickwick. *The Lord of the Rings* is now an institution.

Tolkien believed that fundamental truths were contained within all myths. In writing *The Lord of the Rings* he also attempted to demonstrate that language was inseparable from those myths. The Arthurian tales lead to a greater understanding of human interaction, rules of behaviour, and the purpose of existence. Tolkien also achieves these ends, and his own chronicle of courage, duty, and enchantment evokes a deep response in the human psyche. It does this primarily by the use of symbolism, so well worked into the narrative that all the writing generates an enormous power.

Gandalf, Tolkien's most enduring creation, has much of Merlin about him. His creator described Gandalf as an 'Odinic wanderer', and there is also much of Odin in Merlin. The similarities do not end there. Both Gandalf and Merlin disappear from the scene almost as soon as the company has been assembled, leaving them to fend for themselves. Gandalf must do battle with the Balrog and Merlin set about placating his own inner demons. The indication is that supernatural aid will only be available for a limited time; from then on those who are engaged upon a quest have only themselves to rely upon. No magician can interfere with the fate of the world, either to save it or condemn it.

Magick is forever neutral. The contrast between the magick of Gandalf and that of Sauron, the servant of Mordor, is made very plain. The Elven kingdom of Lothlorien hosts all the enchantment of Middle Earth, and Galadriel,

its queen, aids the Fellowship of the Ring in their task.
Gandalf obviously aligns himself with the fairy power,
and his metamorphosis from 'Gandalf the Grey' to 'Gandalf the White' implies his total alliance with the forces of
light. Sauron is wholly 'dark' and can only be challenged
successfully by a figure that is wholly pure.

Merlin, too, is associated with *elves*, those messengers
of the other world similar to angels. The wizard's role is as
an *interpreter* between the worlds, informing Arthur of the
ways of the cosmos. Merlin's Anglo-Saxon name will be
Rof Breoht Woden (Bright Strength of Woden) and in Elizabethan times he will be *Robin Goodfellow*. Elves are the essence of a timeless world and so much attached to their
surroundings that it is difficult to decide if they made the
land or the land made them. Tolkien's *mise en scène* comes
close to Ragnarok, the Norse apocalypse, which ends with
the triumph of evil over good. Though they know this will
happen, nevertheless the heroes fight on, and to their last
breath—a noble principle. Evil is potentially as powerful
as good, but it suffers from one fatal flaw—it takes itself
too seriously. It has little imagination and no humour.

The Ring demonstrates that owning unlimited personal power is always dangerous. The tragic end of Boromir proves this. So drunk with the idea of power are
the followers of the Dark Lord that the *destruction* of the
Ring is the last course that Mordor expects its enemies to
take. Good champions love and freedom, but it does not
always win; that is the way of things. Given that, good still

believes that embracing evil is not in its nature; if it does embrace evil, good dies. In our world it is often difficult to tell the bad guys from the good ones; that is our present moral dilemma. Maybe it always was the way of things and little has changed over the millennia. One would like to believe that mankind becomes wiser with each succeeding generation, but history demonstrates over and over again that this is not so. It is a constant hope that humanity really *progresses*, but one wonders if we ever do, or ever will.

The magician walks diligently upon his ordained path and does not stray from it. It would be a tragedy if he did, as witness the fallen wizard Saruman in Tolkien's saga. The ways of the magician are hidden from the eyes of others. Magicians are rarely social creatures, for one way that the magus preserves his power is by being alone. He is akin to the megalithic stones that stand as sentinels of space and time, gathering and sustaining the power of the earth. The magician is the most wonderful and loyal companion, yet he never expects anyone to follow him. Neither would he use his will to make another do his bidding.

Flawed though they may be in their earthly incarnation, both Arthur and Merlin are on the side of good. I have felt them both within me, and I have seen their god-like character in other men. That experience has made me almost dumb with awe. Reflecting upon the character of Lancelot and Mordred forces us to see how destiny marks each of us for a particular role. The love of all three of Arthur's queens I have known, too, and I consider that an enlightening experience.

I can only say that an involvement with things Arthurian leads to happenings that are eminently supernatural. As Jung proposed, myth does have a great significance in human consciousness. It nurtures the imagination and leads us into realms where we may know the greatest joy and gain supreme wisdom.

New Age

Values alter, but truths do not. The ancients took great pains to seek out the heart of creation, and modern human beings seem determined to deny that the universe, with all its wonder and unexplained mysteries, actually exists at all. Time travel always appears to be an attractive prospect, particularly if one could embrace a world free of light pollution, sound pollution, and air pollution—a place with no buildings, roads, or vehicles, where silence is broken only by the call of birds and the cry of beasts. This was Britain before the coming of the Romans to our shores. This was the true Albion. It is almost impossible to put oneself into the shoes of those who went before. With the advent of the Aquarian Age, much has been rediscovered that is worthwhile, but we should beware of believing that the hawking of information in itself is our salvation. Understanding is the key to enlightenment, not knowledge for its own sake; that is a sterile approach to learning.

Some associate the New Age with the coming of the Age of Aquarius, but is it the Industrial Revolution that ushers in this era, or more simply the beginning of the twentieth century? Whatever the view, the *New Age* is with us, though to define what it represents is no easy task. The term *New Age* or *New Era* has certainly been used before. Alice Bailey used it in reference to the transition from the age of Pisces to that of Aquarius. It is also likely that thinkers at the beginning of the twentieth century spoke of the coming years in those terms.

To anyone who knew the 1960s, the New Age might just seem to be adding additional verses to a familiar refrain. Images of late-1960s culture range from the revisionist take of an *Austin Powers* movie to exhaustive studies of Marxist schisms in radical politics. The era embraced the *guru*, with a soundtrack to all this meditation and contemplation provided by Ravi Shankar, the masterful exponent of the sitar. Some Sixties philosophies have not aged well, and much New Age philosophy lacks an element of plain old common sense. Wisdom endures, and the old saws were passed on from generation to generation because they could be seen to have a practical application. Magick is essentially a practical science, and it will more than hold its own when faced with any amount of intellectual rigour. If your pet New Age premise can withstand being closely examined and debated, then it will actually feel stronger in your heart. The intuition and the intellect have never been sworn enemies, as some people believe; they are simply two functions of the mind. In magick, polarities are combined to produce a third element—in this particular case, understanding.

Those who aspire to walk the Inner Planes may have an enthusiasm that is boundless, but for reasons of temperament or personal karma many should leave well enough alone. As practitioners, we are all part of the great magickal tradition. Let us make certain magick continues to be a business of wonder and might. Read and study the works of the great and good. I am personally committed to a magickal tradition centering around Dion Fortune; for any student I cannot recommend her writings too highly. A pupil of Dion Fortune, the splendid Christine Hartley, also wrote fine books on magick. The record of her magickal journeys with Charles Seymour demonstrate how much can be achieved by like minds. Her own pupil was Alan Richardson, who, in having Bill Gray as a mentor as well as Christine, made absolutely certain of his magickal antecedents. He too has written extensively of magickal practice and is one who really knows what he is talking about. For those engaged in research on magick, whatever strikes a magickal chord, use or adapt it is my advice.

The path of magick is not for all; it is a way of life, not a hobby. The 'dabbler' is a danger to himself and others, and only the very deluded members of our society consort with him. All of us are at some time shown the path that we should take; whether we choose to walk upon it is our decision and ours only. We are given *free will*; that is part of the agreement the universe has made with humanity. Many use that will to harm themselves and others, but the wise and good do not. The hallmark of those that are chosen to share the divine knowledge is a burgeoning courage. 'To dare' is a brief phrase but awesome in its application. 'To know', 'To will', and 'To be silent', the remaining phrases that make up the quartet, are also pungent with their own power. When the magician practises his art, nothing distracts him from his purpose. He treats his calling with the utmost seriousness, yet he does not take *himself* seriously.

The element of Earth appears to be the least *exciting*. Fire and Water move our passions, Air gives us inspiration, but Earth is regarded as somehow *dull*. It is a false impression, for the earth provides all that nurtures us, and all natural beauty belongs to the material of the planet. The Goddess brings her divine presence to the material when she imbues all with life. She gives us delight and pleasure in all that she provides, and we should give thanks. Instead, many upon this planet abuse her, squander her natural resources, and pollute her seas. Is it not a wonder that with one toss of her golden tresses she does not rid the planet of man, with his arrogance and rapacious ways? She chooses not to take this perfectly just course, but to forgive him—and the holy flowers burst into bloom once more.

In this New Age have the King and the Magus welcomed this renewed interest in all things Arthurian? As the master of the natural world, Merlin is an artist as well as a magician. In the same way that a painter creates a landscape with colour, or a writer brings pictures to the mind, Merlin, working alongside the Goddess, is the creator of form. He is the mortal closest to God that we can know. He has the power to give us paradise and surround us with light and joy. The Sun is in majesty in the Heavens; the music of the waters can be heard for an eternity; and the horizon is forever a distant dream. Merlin employs his ability to make worlds come to life. But Merlin is only too aware of the melancholy tone of the Latin phrase *Et in Arcadia Ego*, meaning that the shadow of death is always present, even in paradise.

Does Merlin believe Art can be a noble compensation? If the artist has a truly visionary approach to his calling, then it is so. The work lives on, long after its creator has become dust, and remains a reminder of his genius. We should be grateful for the dedication and application that has been shown in the work, as we should give thanks for the presence of Merlin in our world. Merlin is true to his calling. The way that he follows is always the true way. We would do well to follow him. The purpose, the only purpose, of magick is to bring light from Heaven above to the earth below. Illumination, whether appearing dramatically in the lightning flash, or more soberly in the light of the Hermit's lantern, represents the magician's purpose.

The Arthuriad is a great, if not the *greatest*, tale that has been taken to the hearts of so many. It is a romantic adventure, a work of philosophy, a moral tale, and a magickal thesis. Merlin, in his greatness, formulated certain occult principles even if there is no record that he was even literate. He is the magician all others have aspired to be whether they realize it or not. Merlin has the ease of the great magus who has merely to desire a change in the material plane for it to happen.

We might ask finally, 'What is the good of magick?' Israel Regardie provides as good an answer as any:

> If it [magick] succeeds in making us better men and women, a little more kind and generous, a little more aware of the spiritual heights to which we are capable of climbing with but a little exertion, then it is the religion of religions . . . surely it is an Art before which all other Muses must bow the head and bend the knee in reverential and perennial praise! [7]

And as for Merlin, let us leave him as he strides along a high mountain pass, climbs a lofty peak, regards the valleys and lakes with a benign eye, and raises his staff on high. Once more he knows that all creation is at his command. We can only imagine the thoughts that run through that extraordinary mind at such a moment. Perhaps none, yet about his lips eternally plays an enigmatic smile.

---

7. Israel Regardie, *The Art and Meaning of Magic*. (Toddington, UK: Helios, 1964).

* Bibliography *

Barber, Richard. *The Holy Grail: Imagination and Belief*. London: Penguin, 2004.

Bradley, Marion Zimmer. *Lady of Avalon*. London: Viking Penguin, 1997.

Bulfinch, Thomas. *Mythology*. New York: T. Y. Crowell Co., 1913.

Castaneda, Carlos. *A Journey to Ixtlan*. London: The Bodley Head, 1972.

Cavendish, Richard. *King Arthur &The Grail: The Arthurian Legends and Their Meaning*. London: Weidenfeld and Nicholson, 1978.

Collins, Andrew. *The Cygnus Mystery*. London: Watkins, 2006.

de Troyes, Chrétien (trans. W. W. Comfort). *Arthurian Romances*. London: Dent, 1958.

Fortune, Dion. *Aspects of Occultism*. Wellingborough, UK: The Aquarian Press, 1962.

———. *The Mystical Qabalah*. New York: Ibis, 1979.

Hutton, Ronald. *Witches, Druids and King Arthur*. London: Hambledon, 2006.

Jung, Emma, and Marie-Louise Von Franz. *The Grail Legend*. Princeton, NJ: Princeton University Press, 1998.

Knight, Gareth. *The Secret Tradition in Arthurian Legend*. Wellingborough, UK: Aquarian Press, 1984.

Malory, Sir Thomas (ed. A. W. Pollard). *Le Morte d'Arthur*. London: Medici Society, 1929.

Mann, Nicholas R. *Energy Secrets of Glastonbury Tor*. Glastonbury, UK: Green Magic, 2004

Michell, John. *The View Over Atlantis*. London: Thames and Hudson, 1983.

Millar, Ronald. *Will the Real King Arthur Please Stand Up?* London: Cassell, 1978.

Regardie, Israel. *The Art and Meaning of Magic*. Toddington, UK: Helios, 1964.

Richardson, Alan. *Priestess: The Life and Magic of Dion Fortune*. Loughborough, UK: Thoth, 2007.

Shippey, Tom. *J. R. R. Tolkien: Author of the Century*. London: HarperCollins, 2001.

Storms, Godfrid. *Anglo-Saxon Magic*. The Hague, Netherlands: Martinus Nijhoff, 1948.

Tennyson, Alfred. *Idylls of the King, and Other Arthurian Poems*. London: Nonesuch, 1968.

Tolstoy, Nikolai. *The Quest for Merlin*. London: Hamish Hamilton, 1985.

To Write to the Author

If you wish to contact the author or would like more information about this book, please write to the author in care of Llewellyn Worldwide and we will forward your request. Both the author and publisher appreciate hearing from you and learning of your enjoyment of this book and how it has helped you. Llewellyn Worldwide cannot guarantee that every letter written to the author can be answered, but all will be forwarded. Please write to:

Gordon Strong
℅ Llewellyn Worldwide
2143 Wooddale Drive. 978-0-7387-1847-7
Woodbury, MN 55125-2989, U.S.A.

Please enclose a self-addressed stamped envelope for reply, or $1.00 to cover costs. If outside the U.S.A., enclose an international postal reply coupon.

 **Free Catalog**

Get the latest information on our body, mind, and spirit products! To receive a **free** copy of Llewellyn's consumer catalog, *New Worlds of Mind & Spirit,* simply call 1-877-NEW-WRLD or visit our website at www.llewellyn.com and click on *New Worlds.*

☽ LLEWELLYN ORDERING INFORMATION

Order Online:
Visit our website at www.llewellyn.com, select your books, and order them on our secure server.

Order by Phone:
- Call toll-free within the U.S. at 1-877-NEW-WRLD (1-877-639-9753). Call toll-free within Canada at 1-866-NEW-WRLD (1-866-639-9753)
- We accept VISA, MasterCard, and American Express

Order by Mail:
Send the full price of your order (MN residents add 6.875% sales tax) in U.S. funds, plus postage & handling to:

> **Llewellyn Worldwide**
> **2143 Wooddale Drive, Dept. 978-0-7387-1847-7**
> **Woodbury, MN 55125-2989**

Postage & Handling:

Standard (U.S., Mexico & Canada). If your order is:
> $24.99 and under, add $4.00
> $25.00 and over, FREE STANDARD SHIPPING

AK, HI, PR: $16.00 for one book plus $3.00 for each additional book.

International Orders (airmail only):
> $16.00 for one book plus $3.00 for each additional book

Orders are processed within 2 business days.
Please allow for normal shipping time. Postage and handling rates subject to change.

The 21 Lessons of Merlyn

A Study in Druid Magic & Lore

Douglas Monroe

For those with an inner drive to touch genuine Druidism—or who feel that the lore of King Arthur touches them personally—*The 21 Lessons of Merlyn* will come as an engrossing adventure and psychological journey into history and magic.

This is a complete introductory course in Celtic Druidism, packaged within the framework of 21 authentic and expanded folk stories/lessons that read like a novel. These lessons, set in Britain circa A.D. 500, depict the training and initiation of the real King Arthur at the hands of the real Merlyn-the-Druid: one of the last great champions of Paganism within the dawning age of Christianity. As you follow the boy Arthur's apprenticeship from his first encounter with Merlyn in the woods, you can study your own program of Druid apprenticeship with the detailed practical ritual applications that follow each story.

These 21 folk tales were collected by the author in England and Wales during a ten-year period; the Druidic teachings are based on the actual, never-before-published 16th-century manuscript entitled *The Book of Pheryllt*.

978-0-87542-496-5, 448 pp., 6 x 9   **$17.95**

The Lost Books of Merlyn

Druid Magic from the Age of Arthur

DOUGLAS MONROE

Initiation and apprenticeship. Since the publication of *The 21 Lessons of Merlyn*, author Douglas Monroe has received more than 20,000 letters requesting his help in touching these two ancient elements in our modern world.

The Lost Books of Merlyn is that guide, and you are the apprentice. Become an active participant in three mythological stories, restored for today's reader from the famous and rare 16th-century Druid text entitled *The Book of Pheryllt*.

A grimoire follows each story that explains the magical elements in the story and provides instructions on how to re-enact the lessons and replicate the rituals. These grimoires are the next best thing to viewing a magician's personal Book of Shadows, which contains knowledge specially reserved for a chosen apprentice.

978-1-56718-471-6, 432 pp., 6 x 9   **$16.95**

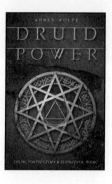

Druid Power

Celtic Faerie Craft & Elemental Magic

AMBER WOLFE

(Formerly titled *Elemental Power*)

Gain greater personal awareness and increased magickal power through the magick of Druidic tradition. *Druid Power* provides groundbreaking methods for self-transformation based on principles and practices of the Celtic Faerie Craft. By teaching spiritual development in the Celtic and Faerie Way, Amber Wolfe blends ancient Celtic ideas with modern psychology.

Readers learn how to reconnect with the natural world through traditional ceremonies, guided imagery, breath work, and other shamanic techniques. Packed with powerful rituals, historical references, and valuable techniques for spiritual growth, *Druid Power* is an invaluable resource for new journeyers or advanced Celticists.

978-0-7387-0588-0, 288 pp., 6 x 9   **$15.95**

When I See the Wild God

Encountering Urban Celtic Witchcraft

LY DE ANGELES

Encounter the God of the Wild Wood.

Magic and witchcraft begin with self-awareness. A crucial step toward self-awareness is recognizing the many faces of the witches' god. This book provides a clear mythology for those who need assistance in answering the call of wildness within.

High Priestess Ly de Angeles teaches beginning and advanced practitioners about the persona of the gods and the Celtic perspective of sacredness. Going beyond ordinary witchcraft manuals, she explains fundamental concepts, such as logos and mythos, the Tuatha Dé Danann, the Quicken Tree, immortality, animism, pantheism, and the elements. Also included are urban stories of magical realism, which take readers on a ritual journey to understanding the solstices and equinoxes.

978-0-7387-0576-7, 240 pp., 6 x 9   **$12.95**

Celtic Magic

D. J. CONWAY

If you have an interest in the ancient Celts and the Celtic pantheon, *Celtic Magic* is the map you need for exploring this ancient and fascinating magical culture.

Celtic Magic is for the reader who is either a beginner or intermediate in the field of magic. It provides an extensive "how-to" of practical spellworking. Many books on the market deal with the Celts and their beliefs, but *Celtic Magic* guides the reader to a practical application of magical knowledge for use in everyday life. There is also an in-depth discussion of Celtic deities and the Celtic way of life and worship, so that an intermediate practitioner can expand upon the spellwork to build a series of magical rituals. Presented in an easy-to-understand format, *Celtic Magic* is for anyone searching for new spells that can be worked immediately, without elaborate or rare materials, and with minimal time and preparation.

978-0-87542-136-0, 224 pp., 4³⁄₁₆ x 6⅞   **$7.99**

Celtic Myth & Magick

Harness the Power of the Gods & Goddesses

EDAIN McCOY

Tap into the mythic power of the Celtic goddesses, gods, heroes, and heroines to aid your spiritual quests and magickal goals. *Celtic Myth & Magick* explains how to use creative ritual and pathworking to align yourself with the energy of these archetypes, whose potent images live deep within your psyche.

Celtic Myth & Magick begins with an overview of 49 different types of Celtic Paganism followed today, then gives specific instructions for evoking and invoking the energy of the Celtic pantheon to channel it toward magickal and spiritual goals and into esbats, sabbats, and life-transition rituals. Three detailed pathworking texts will take you on an inner journey where you'll join forces with the archetypal images of Cuchulain, Queen Maeve, and Merlin the Magician to bring their energies directly into your life. The last half of the book clearly details the energies of over 300 Celtic deities and mythic figures so you can evoke or invoke the appropriate deity to attain a specific goal.

This inspiring, well-researched book will help solitary Pagans who seek to expand the boundaries of their practice to form working partnerships with the Divine.

978-1-56718-661-1, 464 pp., 7 x 10   **$22.95**

Sacred Paths for Modern Men

A Wake Up Call from Your 12 Archetypes

DAGONET DEWR

Dagonet Dewr galvanizes the men's spirituality movement with this much-needed guide to divine masculinity. This book is not just for Pagans, but for men of all faiths who want to explore and learn from their spiritual roots.

With humor and sensitivity, the author introduces twelve male archetypes—including the Child, the Warrior, the Lover, the Healer, and the Trickster—and the gods who embody them. Stories of deities from Pagan lore and mythology spanning several cultures—and even characters from *The Lord of the Rings* and Arthurian literature—offer a rich framework for understanding the heritage of the sacred male. Rituals and magickal workings—for individual or group practice—offer practical ways to connect with these masculine energies and achieve a new understanding of their role in everyday life.

978-0-7387-1252-9, 288 pp ., 5³⁄₁₆ x 8   **$14.95**